Endorsements

Out of the Slave Fields by Bruce Ladebu is an amazing heart-wrenching story. The descriptive language of this book projects images on the heart of the reader that activates compassion for the children and adults who are victims of slavery and sex trafficking. Shocking scenes and incomprehensible living conditions are minor compared to the pain and anguish these precious children and adults experience on a daily basis. The redemptive portion of this book gives hope to the reader as Mr. Ladebu and his team of deliverers rescues many of these slaves from their life of drudgery and hopelessness. This book exposes what has been hidden from most of us, and opens our eyes to the need for compassion for human suffering and the motivation to do something about it.

Regina Shank, CEO
Global Transformation International

Be bold And impact the world!

B

This book will, without a doubt, change your life. Period. ***Out of the Slave Fields: Liberating Children from Brick Kilns and Brothels*** is shocking, yet inspiring, gut-wrenching, yet hopeful. This unequivocally crucial publication should be read and re-read again and again as a reminder for ourselves to not fall into the traps that modern society has fallen into, "growing comfortable to the point of apathy, while slavery has become the very fabric of many economies." Bruce Ladebu, from the depths of my soul, I thank you for this book.

Brian "Head" Welch
co-founder of the
Grammy Award winning band Korn
New York Times best-selling author of
Save Me From Myself

Out of the Slave Fields tells the story of the courageous overseas rescue missions of Bruce Ladebu and his teams. Every mission had one goal: *rescue children*. As I devoured each chapter, I visualized the faces of every broken, oppressed slave. I cried, yelled at the pages, and even chuckled a bit at Bruce and the team's commentary.

If you long to make a difference in the lives of others, then you need to read his book asap! You will learn about the dark reality of modern-day slavery, the inhumane treatment of fellow Christians in other countries, and the everyday heroes who provide justice and freedom to those in debt bondage.

By the end, you will be inspired, compelled, and challenged to make a difference.

Angel Noble
Co-Founder, Mission of Truth

This book is an awakening. High praise for Bruce Ladebu as he drags the darkness into light in this compelling collection of stories that will break your heart and give you hope!

A wake-up call for everyone that reads this compelling truth. Once you have the knowledge you lose the luxury of life as usual. You may not have the ability to physically free the enslaved but we do have the power to support those that are equipped and called to the front line. The Children's Rescue Initiative gives hope to the hopeless.

Mia Perez-Owens
Business Owner

I was floored when I heard about Bruce's mission.

What he does for the children. How he follows what God has called him to do and he does it. He does it without question. The danger he puts himself in blew me away. For the kids. For the babies. He pulls children away from monsters and keeps them safe.

He tells his story humbly. He tells it because God asks him to.

I'm honored to know this man. To be a small part of the safe space he has created. As an avid reader, I will tell you this is one you won't put down easily.

Tayla Lynn
Granddaughter of Loretta Lynn
Singer Songwriter

Not a mere entertaining read, *Out of the Slave Fields* is an eye-opening, gut-wrenching march alongside liberating warriors that you absolutely know God is championing. The book's beauty is the ability to hear the story from the newly liberated individuals and families as well as the (sometimes) well-calculated withdrawal side. Freedom has been taken far too lightly by those of us who have benefited from the many and varied sacrifices of others.

I am grateful for the rescuers who were able to share things from their perspectives. Why they do this, the deep effects and, in some cases, healing they've received as they became a team with the sole goal of redeeming innocent lives that have been stolen.

Be forewarned, this is an action-provoking read. Whether by physical, financial, or spiritual means, you cannot read this and simply do nothing. We all are capable of doing something.

Christine Thompson, author
After the Storm, Still a Promise

This book is written from a God fearing, good man's heart, who's been more places and had more experiences in this life than most. Anyone born with ANY sort of privilege should read this book. This book needs to be read to gain a greater understanding of how the world really is, and to see if God is calling you to help in this work, or to see if it pulls on your heart strings enough to help those who aren't born with privilege, or to help those who just can't help themselves.

Lana Mackey
Co-Owner Adaptive Ops

In his book Out of the Slave Fields, Bruce takes us deeply into personal stories of tragedy and puts a magnifying glass to the systems that enable modern day slavery. You, yourself, as the reader, walk down the dusty pathways of other countries with Bruce and his team, fully armed with vision and action. You meet children that inspire hope and also horrible human adults that will take a life without thought. You toss and turn in your sleep with his team and you find the courage to confront what appear to be insurmountable odds. You are compelled forward towards change as Bruce tackles systems of support that move beyond the doors of freedom – in multiple acts of justice, bravery, and heroism, along with the building of management systems that transport the enslaved to thrive as freed people.

I have known the author, Bruce, for over 30 years as a man of belief, compassion, and action. He has always carried the flags of faith and freedom in his ventures, focused on helping others and connecting them to a deeper faith in themselves and God. On this, the pinnacle of his life's work, Bruce takes us with him to expand our understanding of the harsh world while carrying the flame of love and freedom. You will be forever changed by engaging with this book and will never see the world the same again.

Gardiner Tucker, Ph.D.,
Faculty and Program Director,
Higher Education & Student Affairs Leadership Program,
University of Northern Colorado

Out of the Slave Fields

Liberating Children from
Brick Kilns and Brothels

Bruce Ladebu

Out of the Slave Fields: Liberating Children from Brick Kilns and Brothels

By Bruce Ladebu

Copyright © 2022 Bruce Ladebu

LCCN: 2022922833

ISBNs:
Hardcover 979-8-9874454-1-9
Paperback 979-8-9874454-0-2
eBook 979-8-9874454-2-6

Published by REBEL QUEEN

Front Cover Photo by Pascal Depuhl

Contents

Contents

Acknowledgments

First and foremost, I want to thank my family for their sacrifice while I was gone for long periods of time into dangerous territories.

I want to thank the men and women who have traveled with me on one or more of the rescue operations in Western Asia: Robert, Al, Aaron, Jody, John, Richard, Eric, Joel, Bob, Tom, Rick, Jon, Christian, and my beautiful wife, Aricka. You have been brave champions for the children.

I want to thank all who have financially supported this work of rescuing the slave children. You are a great blessing and crucial to our success!

I also want to thank the unknown warriors who are giving their lives to rescue children. You may never be known for what you are doing, but your reward will be great!

I have used call signs for many of our team members to protect their identities. A special thanks to Catch Dog, Yeti, Minus One Eye, Beast, Click, Cheetah, Rogue, Flex, Hoss, Kaiser, Punda, Gun Smoke, Buddy, and others.

Thank you, Minus One Eye, Yeti, Catch Dog for your contributions to the book. Thank you, Kaiser, Aaron, Josh, and Joelle for your outstanding video and photography work on missions! And thank you, Angel and Jim, for your excellent editing work. Your contributions have been invaluable.

I want to give a special thanks to these heroes, Emanuel and G-man, who risk their lives daily in the pursuit of justice.

To those reading, I hope this book touches your hearts deeply, and that you receive a vision for rescuing the invisible children who are caught in the web of slavery.
Bruce, a.k.a. The Professor

Until I draw my last breath,
I will rescue children.

Bruce Ladebu

Foreword

by Harold Eberle

IN MY TRAVELS AROUND THE WORLD, I encounter children everywhere. Children who are well cared for and loved, and children who are discarded like trash. I've seen children in the Philippines living on a garbage dump, playing soccer with a dead rat for a ball. I've seen children in Holland dressed prim and proper, riding to school perched on their parent's bicycles. I've seen feral street children in South America prey on tourists like a pack of hungry wolves. Everywhere I've gone, I've seen children well-fed and hungry, cherished and scorned, exalted and forgotten. Mostly, though, it's the children I don't see that weigh heaviest on my heart.

Children are resilient. They love unreservedly and forgive readily. They smile quickly, cry heartily, and shrink from danger. They are easily shamed and just as easily restored to joy. Every feeling a child has rushes to the forefront of their visage. They are open; nothing is held back. Everything is freely given and freely received: a kind word, a warm smile, a gentle hug.

A child's heart is pure, the perfect imprint of their creator. They enter this life untouched by the world . . . until the world touches them. And woe to those who do.

I can tell a lot about a culture by how it treats its children, those unblemished lives that rarely have a voice in society. Children are easy to ignore. Oh, I know. Late-night feedings notwithstanding. Let a child cry long enough, however, and he will cease crying. And that, my friends, is where the tragedy begins, for he stops believing that anyone is there.

Bruce Ladebu sees a world that most of us choose to ignore. It is a world both inconvenient and discomforting. *We take care of our own kids. Why bother? Let others take care of theirs.* I wish it was that simple.

Yes, caring for children is engrained in a parent's psyche. Hard work at times, certainly, but instinctual—a part of who we are. Try to come between a mother and her child and tell me how it goes. It's when that bond is severed, however, that we find children adrift, vulnerable, and all too often victimized. This is when they need us to come to their aid.

Nothing is easy about fighting evil, leaving our comfortable homes and daily lives and descending into the abyss of hell that extracts life from children. It is difficult to confront this. . . . But it is easier, in the long run, than ignoring it.

My ministry is active in many of the nations that Bruce and his organization, Children's Rescue Initiative, work in. So, I know whereof he speaks. I have seen the deplorable conditions firsthand. This is why I am honored to lend my voice to his efforts.

A culture that allows its children to be sacrificed for social and economic gain is a culture that will admit entrance to any evil. Ultimately, it will withstand nothing.

My friends, we are that culture. It's not the foreigners in some dark corner of the globe who bear the responsibility for the lost souls of children. It is us. It is up to free people everywhere to help free those enslaved.

Bruce has written a deeply moving account of his work in the slave fields and brothels so we can understand what is going on beneath us. Let him take you there. Let him raise your awareness. It won't always be pleasant, but it is necessary for each of us to find our place in this battle for children and for the future of mankind.

Look around you, past the fine trim lawns, the white fences, the smiling faces and banal conversations. Go beyond your borders. Follow the silence. Ask the questions. Challenge the answers. Look under the covers. Illuminate the darkness.

The defenseless are waiting, hidden in chains, some crying, some silenced. They are waiting for rescue. They are waiting for us.

Prologue

My Story

PEOPLE HAVE OFTEN ASKED ME how I went from a small-town boy in Titusville, Pennsylvania (the historical town where oil was first discovered in America), to running operations all over the world to rescue victims of labor slavery and sex trafficking. Well, it was a long journey. I came from a good family with hard-working parents and great siblings. Even still, I had a lot of problems as a child, mostly because I was being abused by an older girl. Additionally, I figured out early on how to get out of school. I am not sure how I learned it, or exactly why, but I faked sickness so I could stay home from school and read books. In sixth grade, I missed seventy-five days of school. By eighth grade, with my copious amount of reading from home, I became an authority on Jacques Cousteau, marine biology, and oceanography. I liked eighth grade so much, I did it twice!

Even though I was reading volumes, I was terrible in school. Later in life, I realized I was a non-traditional learner. Because I did so poorly in school, I focused on experiential learning, and I learned quickly. At sixteen (in 1971), I drove myself an hour to a scuba school in Erie, PA, and enrolled in a certification course. I had worked hard to make enough money to buy my equipment and pay the tuition. With my parents' help, I was soon ready to explore the underwater world. By the time I was eighteen, I had been diving around shipwrecks, underwater habitats, caves, and a multitude of lakes and sinkholes from the Great Lakes to Nova Scotia to Florida. I did ice diving, night diving, and spearfishing—all by eighteen years old.

My reading and learning experiences launched me into a career as a professional guide and adventurer.

I was very selfish, though, and as a teen, my world revolved around me. I was determined to become a professional diver. Later, in March of 1975, I entered the Air Force to become a Pararescue Specialist (PJ)—to rescue and medically treat downed military personnel all over the world. Unfortunately, my naivety in human nature led me to trust a recruiter who failed to tell me that, with the close of the Vietnam war, the job classification of PJ was closed to new applicants. This intentional oversight landed me squarely into a supply squadron, managing inventory. I was devastated and humbled; I could have found a warehouse job back home. Still, I got to serve my country, so I made the best of it. The good news was that I was stationed at McChord Air Force Base in Washington State, where the outdoor world is amazing. Eventually, through meeting the right people, I soon learned mountaineering and many other skills that would shape the rest of my life.

As my skills grew, I was eventually asked to join a team that was following another group of pararescuers after a C-141 Starlifter crashed in the Olympic Mountains. The plane had received wrong information from the flight tower and dropped below the summit of Inner Constance, hitting it dead on and killing all sixteen on board. Attempts to reach the crash site failed due to inclement weather and dangerous snow conditions. It was late spring before our team could reach it. We spent six weeks securing wreckage and recovering body parts.

Once I left the Air Force, I was hired to run the Wilderness Challenge Program in Titusville for the local high school. For the next three years, I took students on trips that included rock climbing and rappelling, caving, cross-country skiing, survival skills, and rope training. During my tenure, I perfected many skills and met key individuals who helped me get on the right path for my future. At a seminar, I met the famous mountaineer and pioneer, Paul Petzoldt. He invited me on a six-week outdoor leadership course in Wyoming in the Tetons. He became my mentor; I was privileged to learn from this great outdoorsman.

Another individual I was fortunate to meet was Dr. Ivan Jirak. To say he was an interesting man is an understatement. With multiple degrees and years of exploring uncharted territories, he founded the AK Adventure Group in Pittsburgh. He also founded the Explorer's Club of Pittsburgh in 1947 and the Angeda Kimonhon School of Exploratory Sciences in 1971. AK stands for an Inuit phrase, *Angeda Kimonhon*, that means "from every direction, face into the wind." Ivan became another mentor, and it was through him that I embarked on my first arctic expedition.

I took my wife, Aricka, to visit him in Pittsburgh. Knowing he had lived with headhunters in Ecuador—he typically parachuted into the jungle, found a tribe and lived with them for months—I was not surprised to see two cases, each with a shrunken head, in his living room. Aricka, however, needed a little convincing regarding their scientific purpose.

Later, I joined Dr. Jirak on the East of North Expedition to Bylot Island, a mostly-unexplored mountainous island off the north coast of Baffin Island—the largest island in Canada. For two weeks, two teams explored different areas of the island. We also got to name peaks and other landmarks, as we were the first to ever set foot there. (You can read more of these adventures in my upcoming autobiography.)

A year later, I was invited to join the Canadian North Pole Expedition, an attempt to reach the northern pole by human means alone—no air support, no dog sleds or snowmobiles, only human power. The temperature was -70°F and the ice was treacherous. The trip did not succeed, however, as I got sick from a virus I acquired while traveling to Canada. (I suspect a bad batch of Moosehead beer.)

Five years later, Kent Armstrong and I started an outdoor adventure company that led people to various adventure sports and nature courses. During that time, Kent and I, along with others, spent four winters in the backcountry of the Canadian Rockies, filming and photographing wolves and other wildlife. We worked hard and took hundreds of pictures of wolves in the wild. On one occasion, I found myself in the midst of a pack of wolves. Sensing no immediate danger, I tilted my head and howled. The alpha male howled in reply. Soon the entire pack was howling, and we howled together for fifteen minutes.

Cocking their heads to my strange rendition of their plaintive wails, their faces said it all: *How does he stay upright for so long?*

It's a question I ask myself daily.

Introduction

Souls and Statistics

In giving freedom to the slave, we assure freedom to the free—honorable alike in what we give, and what we preserve. We shall nobly save, or meanly lose, the last best hope of earth. Other means may succeed; this could not fail. The way is plain, peaceful, generous, just—a way which, if followed, the world will forever applaud, and God must forever bless.

Abraham Lincoln
Second Annual Message to Congress
December 1, 1862

IN THE COURSE OF MY LIFETIME, I have traveled as a professional adventurer, guide, and explorer to some of the wildest places on earth. These adventures opened my eyes to the world of need that few who stay in the confines of tourist travel ever see. Beyond the nice hotels and tourist attractions, I have found an education immersed in real cultures. I have experienced humanity—the good, the bad, and the ugly. In my journeys around the globe, I have stayed in mud huts in Africa, igloos in the extreme north, cabins in the wilderness, private homes, and hotels ranging from opulent five-star habitations to nasty, cockroach-in-fested dives.

While there are immeasurably good things in the world, there is also human suffering everywhere, surrounded by the perpetrators of the suffering. Whether it is among remote peoples of the wilderness or in cultures elsewhere and beyond, the most tragic suffering is that of children.

Slavery is one of the most lucrative businesses in the world. According to California's Office of the Attorney General, "Human trafficking is among the world's fastest growing criminal enterprises and is estimated to be a $150 billion-a-year global industry."[1]

Slavery is a reality of the modern world. It has existed since the early days of man, and is more prevalent now than at any other time in history. The International Labour Organization states that (as of 2021) there are fifty million slaves living in suffering.[2] I believe this figure is actually higher, considering that in India alone (as of 2016) there are 18.3 million people in some sort of slave labor or debt bondage.[3] UNICEF estimates that in south Asia alone, over forty-one million children are engaged in various forms of child labor.[4] These children face a daily struggle working in brickfields, textile factories, rope plants, cigarette factories—anywhere labor is needed. All over the world, children are forced to do adult-strength labor without much food or water. Child labor and slavery are an everyday part

---

[1] https://oag.ca.gov/human-trafficking
[2] https://www.ilo.org/global/about-the-ilo/newsroom/news/WCMS_855019/
[3] https://www.globalslaveryindex.org/2018/findings/country-studies/india/
[4] https://www.unicef.org/rosa/what-we-do/child-protection/child-labour-and-exploitation

of economic and social life. Entire cultures operate this way, especially in Asia and the Middle East.

In the early nineties, I was asked to join my close friend Dale, who wanted to journey into the former Soviet countries as a missionary. I accepted the offer, and we began a remarkable journey that would take us across ten countries in Europe and eastern Europe. It was in Ukraine that I was first told how girls are forced into the nightmare of sex trafficking.

On a subsequent trip to Pakistan, I personally witnessed modern-day slavery. Not just a few cases, but thousands of people forced into labor or sex work, as young as three to as old as eighty-five. Prior to this, such barbarism was unthinkable—the trafficking of human beings! In that moment, something within me changed. I would never be the same, nor would I ever want to be. I knew I had to do something.

In traveling the world, and through many interviews with natives, I have discovered that minority groups, such as Christians and Hindus in Pakistan, and Uyghurs in China, are intentionally kept in poverty. This creates an ongoing labor pool for slave owners and others seeking workers. Impoverished parents are often forced to sell a child to feed the rest of the family. If slave labor were shut down in some countries, their economies would suffer. Many private homes have slave children doing household chores and other unsavory labor; many are sexually abused.

In countries where social services are weak or non-existent, human traffickers prowl poor areas immediately after a natural disaster—events like earthquakes, floods, and fires—and prey on newly orphaned children for use in local brothels or sales overseas.

This nightmare is occurring every second of every day in every country in the world.

In the early nineties, when I started my research into slavery and human trafficking, information was nearly non-existent. Today, statistics on the subject are readily available, to the extent that we easily become numb to the subject. What difference does it make to the average person whether there are four million slaves or five million slaves in Pakistan? We in the West are busy taking our kids to school, rushing to work, and struggling to pay our bills. When confronted with the tragedy of slavery, we hope someone else is working on these other problems. Statistics too easily became soulless numbers replacing human beings.

For this reason, I will focus primarily on my personal experiences in freeing human slaves. I want to put a face on every number, a story behind every click of a statistician's calculator. These figures represent human beings, after all—both the victims and the perpetrators. That is why parts of these stories will be difficult to read. I humbly ask, however, that you stay with them. Shock and awe are not my goals. Instead, I want to enlighten you and hopefully enlist you. . .in some fashion. The needs are varied, the challenges daunting.

To liberate victims, one must make the journey into enemy territory and bring back the treasures the perpetrators took captive. It is not easy being on the front lines, but to not go is almost as criminal as the perpetrators themselves. Many of my team members are former military.

They know how to operate in hostile environments, how to read a situation, and how to apply judicious force toward a targeted end. As of this writing, my teams and I have freed thousands of children and adults from the hell of labor and sex slavery. In addition, we have directly influenced the rescuing of thousands more through individuals and organizations that we support, along with being advisors to others over the years.

Throughout this journey, my teams and I have learned the wrong ways and the right ways to free slaves in the darkest corners of the world. At times, my revulsion over what I've witnessed has tempted me to eliminate some decadent lives. Thankfully, I have stayed within proper parameters to avoid providing any ember the enemy can fan into flames of persecution. Minority groups in various nations have already endured their villages being destroyed and the killing of those whom the government deemed justifiable. The skill in what we do involves pushing the limits in the midst of hell without causing an uprising or breaking laws. We go as far as we can to release as many souls as possible. In the process, we have angered powerful people. So be it. My Asian Director of Operations and I have had contracts out on our lives. He eventually had to flee his native country with his family due to the Taliban's attempting to kill him.

Becoming actively involved in freeing these victims of terror has changed my life, and thankfully, the lives of thousands of children and adults. Partnering with other talented abolitionists, our work has taken us into some of the most dangerous territories on planet Earth. We have faced terrible people, risking our lives to accomplish what has become the stories in this book.

Learning how to effectively rescue the enslaved has been a major learning curve for me. I started out by buying slaves at prevailing rates. While this freed the immediate slave(s), the slavers merely took my money and bought new ones. Thus, I quickly learned to negotiate ten cents on the dollar. The slavers didn't like it, but my team and I learned to make offers they couldn't refuse. Finally, we just went in and took them. (More on that later.)

We made many mistakes, as we had no one to learn from. But we improved with each mission, evolving from mere conversations to negotiating, to getting radical. One time, we entered a brick kiln—a brick factory where slaves make bricks by hand—and discovered the owner and his main guys were not there. As quickly as we could, we loaded up eighty slaves and drove off. Realizing that this was even possible was a revelation to my team and the local abolitionists we worked with.

Rescuing slaves has always been dangerous, costly work, but the result of the brave men and women who have worked with me is that several thousand human beings have been set free. Our work will continue, and we expect to rescue thousands more.

The stories in this book take place between 2009 and 2020. They represent a progression. On each journey, we learned how to do our rescues better. Finally, in 2018, we found new levels of excellence. Along the way, we partnered with amazing people and gained incredible new team members—becoming the professional force we are today.

One disclaimer, however. Over the years, my teams and I have participated in over 125 rescues. It is natural, therefore, that some details have become blurred. Other details have been deliberately obscured to protect the participants. Finally, we have combined some stories to present a composite whole—a readable narrative.

Those who know me will tell you I'm a plain-spoken man. This book follows that pattern—very little is held back. I have written sincerely and honestly about this hidden modern-day tragedy and the societies that allow it to fester. My heart is broken for those who have no voice and must endure unspeakable crimes against them. As a result of the horrors of slavery, some stories will be hard to read, but you need to know the truth of what is happening in the world.

You need to know the stories of the rescues and redemptions.

You need to know what remains to be done.

To do justice to the fatherless and the oppressed,
That the man of the earth may oppress no more.

Psalms

PART I
Into the Brick Kilns

We're here to help the slave families and put their children in school.

No! Not only do the parents have to work, but their children too. They must pay off their debt!

No child can work under the age of fourteen. This is the law of your government; it's from the Supreme Court! These children are hardly ten years old.

I don't care about the law.

We've been meeting with the highest officials, the police, even the secret police. They support us in rescuing these children.

I don't care about the government. Do you see them here? Of course not! Children must work.

Look at them! They're little. They have no power to work.

These children are my slaves. They will work. We will make them.

We're going to take them back to freedom.

If you want to take them, pay off all their debts. The whole family has to work. They are mine! They have to pay.

It is under the Constitution that no child under the age of fourteen will work.

Why don't you finish their work? Then you can have them! Get out of here before I buy you!

I really want to kill this bastard.

1

Where Are the Champions?

And maybe just remind the few,
if ill of us they speak,
that we are all that stands between
the monsters and the weak.

Michael Marks

BECOMING A CHAMPION requires one thing: desire. On the heels of desire must come pursuit. And pursuit, driven by desire, will result in achievement. I believe that in these times, locked within certain individuals is a desire to be liberators, a drive to rescue innocents from the terrifying existence endured in slavery. These people have *rescue* in their DNA.

For several years after my initial time in the former Soviet countries—knowing that helpless children were being victimized—I couldn't sleep at night. One episode burns in my mind.

I was flying into Ukraine from Europe in 2003 on my way to meet Dale for a follow-up trip to Ukraine. We'd been working together since our first trip in 1993. Across the aisle was a man in his mid-twenties, and beside him was a teenage girl. She giggled a lot, and he had that look of lust in his eyes. I knew little of the world of human trafficking

5

back then. But . . . something was wrong. I watched closely, trying to figure out what it was. They looked at pictures on his camera; sometimes he leaned over her, somewhat concealing her. *Something is off here.* I was traveling alone. The plane was filled with a rough crowd, perhaps Russian Mafia. I wasn't sure.

As we exited the plane, I followed the man and the girl. After they went through customs, they approached a waiting car where the man became a little rough with the girl, pushed her inside the vehicle, hopped in behind her and it sped off. I wasn't sure what I witnessed, but it haunted me.

A Ukrainian Champion

Dale and I were scheduled to meet with a remarkable man known as Pastor Gennady, a champion of the children, who was rescuing boys and girls off the streets. He took us to the city underground to confront a dark, horrifying reality. In a decrepit building, we crawled through a small hole in a wall and entered a space about eight feet by eight feet. Sewage permeated the air. The space had four large pipes running through it and an open trough in the floor flowing with raw excrement. The pipes, only two feet above the trough, had a few blankets laid on them with some personal items on top. The pastor explained that children lived throughout this sewer system and slept above the floor on the pipes. He showed us syringes lying in a corner. The kids made homemade drugs and injected them, often resulting in a flesh-eating bacterial skin condition.

We continued the journey through other buildings and tunnels. A few hours later, we arrived at his home for children. It was a simple house with one large bedroom where children slept in bunks. A woodstove occupied the main room. There were no creature comforts other than wooden chairs and benches. The first child we approached was lying on a bed. He was a pale, gaunt boy of about thirteen. Open sores covered his arms. The pastor said he had the flesh-eating bacterium, and without a miracle he would die. Our host told us that all of the boys in his home live on the streets, are used for sex, eventually fall ill, and end up in his care. With no funds to pay for treatment, the hospital turns them away. The pastor can only pray for them, comfort them and believe in God for miracles.

At the time of my visit, it is estimated[5] that thousands of children lived on the streets in Ukraine. These children were victims of abuse, trafficking, rape, and many other crimes perpetrated by individuals and organizations.

Pastor Gennady told us a thriving market exists for buying and selling children as property. Recruiters offer to take children to new jobs. These kids think they are finally employed, able to help their families, and are on their way to a better life. Instead, they are thrown into the world of sex slavery. A friend of mine witnessed a line of cages with bound girls being bought and sold. Men got out of their cars, felt the merchandise, made a purchase, and the girl was never heard from again.

My heart broke. Were they missed? Was anyone looking for them? Did locals know this was happening right in their communities? We later found out that everyone knew

---

[5] Pace, G. T. (2012). Street children in Ukraine: Homelessness and other associated risks. Journal of Global Awareness, 12, 65-71. https://osf.io/ev5pa/download/

what was going on, but no one had the ability to stop it. What I witnessed during this trip was another catalyst for my passion for rescuing children from a life where they are considered nothing more than animals.

Where are the champions? Where are the strong, patient, passionate world changers?

Where are the champions?

Perhaps you?

Every great dream begins with a dreamer. Always remember, you have within you the strength, the patience, and the passion to reach for the stars to change the world.

Author Unknown

2

The Making of a Hero

EMANUEL PULLED HIMSELF UP, brushed off his pants, and looked at the small rip in his shirt. *It will mend.* The voices of his tormentors rang in his ears. Almost daily, he ran into this group of boys who beat up the minority children along the route to school. He lost count of the number of times he had been beaten. Emanuel was a Christian, part of a persecuted minority in the nation of Pakistan. Making matters worse, he was light skinned, with dark curly hair. A fighter at heart, he wanted to fight back. He was growing faster and bigger than most boys his age and could have handled himself easily, but the consequences of violence would have been disastrous to his family and his community.

Emanuel's brother and sister had it somewhat easier; they had their dad's favor. Growing up, Emanuel's father was harder on him and emotionally distant, although his mother loved him deeply.

Emanuel grew tall and developed a strength that comes through adversity. Although he was poor and part of the subjugated Christian community, he was able to attend high school and receive higher education after that. He had a gift for languages, speaking over a dozen—many fluently. As an adult, Emanuel used his gifts to develop his

9

ministry. Within this difficult nation, he soon became one of its top Christian leaders. He met with members of parliament, governors, and even the president several times to plead the cause of the minorities within Pakistan.

His was not an easy life. Emanuel was known as a strong leader in his nation. He had the heart of a warrior and the wounds to prove it. During his thirty years of speaking out for the oppressed, he had been stabbed, beaten, shot, jailed, and persecuted by those who hated what he stood for—freedom and justice. Anytime a minority village was burned, Christians killed, or young girls kidnapped for sexual trafficking, Emanuel was on the scene in protest. He even helped in some high-profile legal battles of women accused of heresy—a common legal tactic of the Muslim majority.

It was common for members of the majority to frame Christians for heresy as a form of revenge. In one famous case, an illiterate woman was given a bag of trash to burn. At the last minute, a member of the clergy rushed forth and loudly accused her of defacing the sacred book. A crowd formed, the trash was examined, and a few pages of the book were found in the pile she was about to ignite. A riot ensued. The police arrived just in time to arrest this bewildered woman, thus saving her life. Later that day, in a rare victory for the minority, a copy of a sacred document with the same pages torn out was found in the property of the accusing cleric. Still, the woman served a long prison term while her case was battled in the courts and on the streets. She was eventually released to another country under cover of night as rioting crowds filled the streets to demand her execution. Such a favorable outcome was rare. Christians were usually beaten or burned to death by outraged mobs.

In 2008, Emanuel found me through social media and invited me to Pakistan to teach at a leadership conference. I was hesitant. Pakistan is one of the most dangerous countries on earth. It's a poor country, and deception abounds in such overtures. Through eighteen months' worth of correspondence and what seemed like a thousand questions from me, however, I determined that Emanuel was legit, and I accepted his invitation.

My arrival changed life completely, both for Emanuel and for me. Through a series of unforeseen events, what he thought was impossible became a reality. This is that story.

Emanuel was *and is* a hero to the children of his nation.

Two boys just rescued from a brick kiln get washed off
with help from team members.

3

Ring of Fire

2009—Children's Rescue Initiative

Stand strong against evil. We live in a day and age where we need committed champions— compelled and courageous—whose cause is to bring justice where darkness invades.

Bruce Ladebu

Slave /slāv/ noun – a person who is the legal property of another and is forced to obey them.

Dad / dad / noun – a term of endearment in Pakistan.

*****

ARRIVING IN PAKISTAN FOR THE FIRST TIME was something I never thought would happen. Really, I never wanted to be there. Over the years as a professional adventurer, I had been to dozens of countries, immersed myself in many cultures, and mined the obscure byways far from the weary tourist paths. And while there were many places I had yet to visit, Pakistan never occurred to me as a viable destination until a stranger named Emanuel invited me to hold a leader's conference and speak at a large Christian festival. I spent a year and a half considering his invitation, getting to know Emanuel and evaluating his authenticity through text and email, all the while hoping that my evaluation was accurate. I did not want to be involved in some elaborate criminal scheme to relieve a dumb American of his hard-won cash. Eventually, Emanuel won me over. I decided to trust him, and I saw this conference as an opportunity to deliver a message of hope to his persecuted people.

It was 2 a.m. when I—along with two intrepid volunteers, Robert and Al—rolled through airport security. The official avoided eye contact and instead, stared right through me.

"Passport."

"I see you have your visa."

"Why are you in our country?"

"How long will you be here?"

"Who are you staying with?"

With every question, his invasion of my soul intensified. Finally, he paused as if deliberating, let out a heavy sigh, and stamped the passport without looking down. He did the same to my teammates.

Robert and Al were pastors whom I had recruited to join me on this maiden voyage. Robert was a loving, kind, soft-spoken soul who made friends easily—a man of the heart. A former cross-country runner, he still moved with the lithe grace of one accustomed to being in lean physical shape. His desire to help people was genuine, and he jumped at the opportunity when he heard I was coming to Pakistan to host a religious convention.

Al was tall; he towered over many of the Pakistanis around us. He had a quiet disposition that could explode with spontaneity. I loved Al for his humor, his trademark grin, and his unquenchable hope for all things humanity. I especially treasured his unobtrusive personality. He didn't need the spotlight in order to shine, and fit seamlessly into any human interaction. Still, Al's conditioning concerned me. He had been a tennis player for most of his life, but like his thinning hair, he was drifting toward the softer edges of an easier existence.

I felt ready for whatever lay ahead. I was reasonably fit, had a smattering of martial arts training, and possessed the height advantage that could cast a commanding shadow over anyone in this malnourished society. In my world travels encountering cultures vastly different from my own, I felt confident I could handle myself in any environment, no matter how hostile. Well. . .I guess naivete is a kind of preparation, right?

Before we left, I stressed to both men that Pakistan was a hostile environment in more ways than just spiritual. Staggering heat, biting insects, scorching winds, a merciless sun, and pathogens that even penicillin was scared of—all could take their toll on the fittest of humans. Robert and Al seemed energized by the challenge, and they assured me they were up for the rigors of the trip. I wanted to believe them. Truth be told, I needed Robert and Al like Moses needed Aaron.

While my sleep-addled mind was coming to grips with the sudden shift in time zones, we cleared security, passed through the barriers rimmed with armed guards, and looked into the waiting crowd. A tall, light-skinned Pakistani man standing near the front smiled at me.

Emanuel embraced each of us and placed leis of roses over our heads. I was immediately drawn to his professional demeanor. Having never met in person, we took stock of each other. Emanuel was a broad-shouldered man, alert as a pirate, and possessed burning, resolute eyes. But for his light complexion, he was every inch a Pakistani—meticulously groomed with the requisite mustache, collared shirt, khaki pants, and leather sandals. We both knew we had an instant connection. Overshadowing every other impression at that moment, however, was Emanuel's intensity to get us moving out of the airport and into a waiting van. *We can't stand still for a moment, Emanuel? Where's the danger?*

A team of four men in military gear met us outside the terminal building. They silently surrounded our group and hustled us to the parking lot. The air had an acidic odor that burned my nostrils. Robert winced, and Al sneezed. Both grew quiet, their boisterous optimism from the flight fading. The parking lot lights, shining through dust, cast a yellow pall on everything.

Arriving at the car, the silent sentinels sprang to life. With clicks and whirs like transformers preparing for war, semi-automatic weapons appeared in their hands. Assuming tactical stances, they scanned the horizon for unseen threats. *Exactly how bad is it in this country if people have to travel with armed security?*

My protective nature went immediately to Robert and Al. I admired the courage of these men—both excellent teachers eager to bless a world as far from their own as one could find on this big blue planet. Not many would come to Pakistan without a reason and a deep calling. And yet, while I was trained in operational readiness—an occupational requirement for someone who led worldwide adventures—I suddenly realized we would not last five minutes alone in what passes for everyday life in the rougher parts of this beautiful country. Clearly, we had arrived at the harvest field of our dreams. Now we merely had to survive it.

This was the start of our training in being guarded by personal security. I looked these men over to see if they were ex-military or just some jokers with guns. One man, Yousuf, was definitely trained. I could tell by the way he stood, how he held his weapon and studied his surroundings. His thick mustache and dark, darting eyes looked like a character out of an Indiana Jones movie. All business and no smiles, he would be a serious contender in a fight. I wasn't yet sure about the other armed escorts, but they were in a better position to fight than we were at the moment. Robert, Al, and I squeezed into the back seat, and we set off on a journey that would change our lives.

The two-hour drive was not unpleasant, even though we were exhausted. Emanuel explained that we took a longer route because the quickest route had bandits this time of night. They set up makeshift roadblocks for cash or "stop and rob." Arriving at his home bone-weary, we were greeted by Emanuel's entire family. We exchanged customary greetings, were ushered to our bedrooms, and fell unconscious.

I woke up the next morning, donned my lightweight clothing, and made my way to the living area. The dry air was superheated. I found myself breathing to gain more oxygen, each breath burning my lungs. The sky was haze blue, the sun filtered by the pollution of unrestrained industrial growth, and the sound of motors competing for space on chaotic roads was everywhere.

I knew we'd get used to it—the air, the noise, the humidity—but it was a disconcerting first impression. The redeeming factor at the moment was a wonderful breakfast laid out before me: eggs, mysterious hot sauce, and a tortilla-like bread. Emanuel, Robert, Al, and I ate and talked about the upcoming festival—our leader's conference—and the children of the area. There was so much need in this community. Minorities lived in squalor, beset by poverty, prejudice, and hopelessness. Few employers hire Christians in this Muslim country. Your religion is required on all job applications. Checking the box marked "Christian" diminishes your chances of any consideration.

As we talked, Emanuel told us of the slaves working the brick kilns and factories. Although I had traveled worldwide and had seen unspeakable things, I had a hard time believing there could be tens of thousands of children enslaved in hard labor. I had done a lot of research on Pakistan before we left. Even though it was 2009, there was not a lot of information on modern slavery. Because of the lack of media attention, most people denied that slavery was a reality in the 21st century. Although I believed Emanuel—I wouldn't have been there if I didn't—*seeing is believing.*

"Where are these children? Are they nearby?" I asked.

"Yes, Dad. There is a textile factory just on the other side of these houses."

"Can we go now?"

"Right now, Dad?"

My look said everything.

Emanuel uttered something in Urdu to a staff member who jumped to life. Walking to the car gave us our first indication of the temperatures for the day. It was 45°C. My mind did the math. *Holy cow! It's 113°F!*

Driving a mere half mile, we pulled up to a stone wall with a large cement building behind it. Walking on red dirt that puffed with each step, we followed Emanuel through an archway and into a small courtyard. On a cement bench sat an old woman with a young boy about eight or nine years old. Their heads were down. The woman was speaking quietly to the boy, leaning close to his ear. She wore a traditional white sari, and the boy wore a dirty polo shirt, brown pants, and sandals. We walked past them and entered the open-fronted building unchallenged.

We saw a room full of machines the size of refrigerators. It reminded me of machinery I had seen in tool shops in the United States. The walls were cement and brick, painted blue, chipped, and tattered. Hot oil and fumes filled the air. Two boys stood working at one of the machines. Their faces were covered with dirt and grease. They looked up quickly as we entered, and just as quickly put their heads back down.

"Are these slave boys?" I asked Emanuel over the electric whirr of the motors.

"Yes, Dad. They were bought by the owners. They work here, live here, and probably will die here."

I studied the boys, appalled at their plight. The grim expressions of my companions said they felt the same. We were staring into the face of modern-day slavery, and it was staring back at us.

"Come. There's more," said Emanuel.

We followed him into another room of large machines for weaving cloth. A boy who was about fifteen years old worked alone in a corner. We walked through more rooms and saw several other boys toiling at different stations. Exploring the rest of the factory and marveling that we could move unhindered, we returned to where we started.

A man with sunken, shallow eyes and an evil glint walked up to us. I stared back at him, struggling with an instant dislike of this creature.

"Dad, please meet the owner," said Emanuel.

The slave owner motioned us to a room. We followed, not out of etiquette but from a numb sense of unbelief. Robert motioned to a boy behind the machines with the other boys. He was cleaner than the others, with a bit more flesh on his bones, and he seemed unsure of himself.

"Bruce, that's the kid who was outside on the bench with the old woman," said Robert, pain in his voice.

The boy looked scared. I wasn't sure what was going on, but I intended to find out. Our brief interview with the slave owner only hardened my resolve. He was arrogant in answering our questions. Forced labor was just a part of life in this country as far as he was concerned, and we could go back where we came from if we didn't like it.

As we left through the same courtyard, I asked, "Emanuel, who was that woman and the boy?"

"Sadly, that mother just sold her son to the factory."

"What? Sold him? How could she? Why?"

Emanuel looked at me through tears. "This is a lost generation of Christians. They are so poor; they do this to survive."

"How could any parent sell a child?" Al demanded.

"They sell one to save the rest."

I was dumbfounded. I thought of my children back home, of all the times we struggled to make ends meet. Never in my furthest thoughts had I ever considered selling one of my children.

"Emanuel, I want you to find out how much that little boy was sold for, and we'll get him back!" I said firmly.

"Dad, nobody does that," Emanuel said, shaking his head.

"Well, we are going to do it! This is. . .it's ungodly!"

"Dad, let's go back home and you can think about it. There is much to see in Pakistan, so much to learn. Many, many children are enslaved here. You have seen . . .one."

"Yes, Emanuel, one. And that's how we'll free them— one at a time."

We arrived back at Emanuel's home emotionally drained and needing to rest for the festival later in the day. Adding to the heat and the cultural shift, we were also adjusting to an eleven-hour time difference. While we rested, Emanuel sent someone with money to get the boy and arranged for a foster home. To my knowledge, our first freed slave has been growing and thriving in freedom ever since.

As evening approached, we were taken to the festival grounds where we waited as busload after busload of people arrived. For the next two nights, thousands of people heard Al and Robert open in prayer and then me speak on freedom and equality. During our speeches, I noticed many dirty children in ragged clothing standing eagerly in the front rows. On the last night, I motioned for them to come closer. Several ran away, but two boys stayed. Through an interpreter, I found out their names were Faisal and Jacob. They were slave boys who worked at a local rope factory.

At the end of the festival, the boys followed me to Emanuel's home. I walked Faisal and Jacob over to Emanuel and said, "Emanuel, meet Faisal. He is your new son! And this is Jacob, we will rescue him also."

Emanuel met me with a stone-cold stare.

"No, Dad. I cannot do this."

Our eyes locked.

"This is not done here. It is too dangerous. You do not know these boys. You do not know what they are capable of."

He was adamant. So was I.

"We cannot let them go back," I said, clearly testing the strength of our nascent partnership.

"Dad, we can help the slaves. We can bring them food, water, and get them medical care. But we cannot rescue them. There are too many, and our homes are too small."

"I think we can, Emanuel. We have to."

Emanuel stared at me for a long time and shrugged. I felt the atmosphere shift.

"Okay, Dad. I understand."

Emanuel gave Faisal a hug, took him over to his wife, and had a conversation with her in Urdu. Then I walked Jacob over to Emanuel, leaned close to his ear, and said, "Emanuel, meet your second son."

"Dad! No! I cannot do this!" Emanuel exclaimed.

"Why not?"

"I have no room," he pleaded.

"Emanuel, you must be a rescuer of these children. As a mentor and father figure, I will help you."

"Dad, we could be killed for doing this." Then added softly, "But. . .I am willing to be martyred if needed."

Emanuel sent Faisal and Jacob off for a much-needed shower, and we sat at the long family table on Emanuel's open-air porch. Ropes held heavy curtains back—they could be pulled closed in case of rain or dust storms. Over a meal of curry chicken, rice, and several unknown foods, Robert, Al, Emanuel, and I discussed the horrendous reality of slavery that permeated this country—a malevolent thief robbing thousands of their childhoods. Eating with conviction was Faisal who was fresh from his shower. It was his first full hot meal in his life. He was enjoying his new home.

It was there at this table that we discussed a strategy to free these children.

I glanced at Jacob who had exited the shower room in the new clothing he'd been given and was walking across the courtyard. *I'll bet this is the first shower he's ever taken. Probably the first time he's seen a toilet or a sink too.* Jacob walked to the table and stared at the food. Emanuel's wife, Sara, took him by the hand and showed him how to fill his plate from the serving trays.

We went to our rooms that night with mixed feelings, anticipating what tomorrow would bring. We were going into the slave fields. That's all I knew. I did not sleep well.

Still hammered with jet lag, I exited my room the next morning and greeted the blast furnace that is Pakistan. The temperature was to hit 115°F this afternoon. Our schedule for the morning included speaking at a conference where one thousand attendees were expected to pack into a non-air-conditioned building. In sweltering heat, we spoke and taught strategies for leadership. I could have just as easily taught how to survive in the Sahara. Thoroughly exhausted and soaked to our skin, we waited for the go-ahead from Emanuel to visit the slave field. Though I've seen many difficult things over the years in my journeys around the world, I had this feeling in the pit of my stomach that I was about to enter a world that was going to be more than my mind could comprehend. I had seen many horrible sights: homeless children, children dying from Chernobyl radiation, indescribable poverty, and wanton violence. In my first three days exploring Pakistan, I learned that their economy was influenced strongly by slave labor.

As evening approached, our team gathered and walked a short distance to a rope factory. It was a simple, long, and narrow brick structure with six or seven boys running back and forth carrying very long strings. The boys raced with strings in hand and attached them to a hook where the machine braided them into a rope. Emanuel told us that the boys worked like this for twelve hours a day and were given no food or water.

"How do they eat and drink?" we asked.

"Most slaves must beg for food, and they drink wherever they find water, like a pool of water on the ground!" Emanuel exclaimed. "And these owners beat the children every day. Dad, this is not right for children to be treated like animals. Many of them rape the girls when they reach puberty— or before."

24

It was right there, in this sweltering hell-hole of a rope factory, that something happened inside me that would change my life and the lives of many slave children forever. My heart broke for the children. I was angry at the injustice, helpless in my naivete, guilty for my blindness, and convicted that I needed to do something.

The next day at Emanuel's house, two little girls kept appearing in the courtyard. They smiled at the strange-looking men. We asked them their names. They said "Aabish" and "Maali," then ran away. That night, I had a dream that these precious girls were sold into slavery. During breakfast the following morning, I told Emanuel my concern for those two girls.

"Why, Dad?"

"Emanuel, you must take these girls into your home."

"No, Dad, I cannot. Really, this is too much! We already have the two boys."

"Emanuel, I had a dream last night that these girls are going to be sold into slavery. You already found a home for the boy we rescued at the first factory. You can find homes for these."

Emanuel let out a heavy sigh. "Okay, I will do this," he said.

Through his contacts, Emanuel discovered that the girls' mother was a prostitute. She intended to sell the girls soon, which wouldn't be good for them. And that is how Aabish and Maali, ages five and seven, came to be among the rescued children. We brought them into Emanuel's home where they would be safe. We also promised to help the mother with food. Several months later, she got her life somewhat turned around. The girls visited her but remained with Emanuel's family.

It was time to return to the United States. Robert, Al, and I sat with Emanuel's family and the children we had rescued during our short stay. I kept looking at Faisal. This boy was a slave a few weeks ago, and now he was free. I studied his handsome features as he looked down at new sandals—the first pair he had ever owned. He was free; he would grow up free, and I knew he would work to free others.

I came to this country to lead conferences. I was leaving illuminated to the true mission of my life. With nothing more than a burning conviction in my heart, I knew I must return. My work was far from finished; it had only just begun.

A smiling Faisal watched as we loaded the car. The three of us were tearing up as we pulled away. Faisal ran alongside the car for one hundred yards on the little dirt road, yelling in just-learned English, "I love you. I love you!" Our hearts broke. If one freed slave could run alongside us, how far could I run alongside the slaves?

"I love you too, Faisal," I yelled.

At that moment, I knew I would spend the rest of my life working to save children.

Back home, I went to work creating a non-profit organization, a tax-deductible way for people to support our rescue efforts. I called it *Children's Rescue Initiative*, or CRI for short. I created newsletters and spoke on our mission and vision. Everyone I talked to said the same thing: "I did not know slavery still existed." A few added, "How can I help?" Once I showed pictures and told stories of modern slavery, people got behind the cause.

On the other side of the pond, Emanuel set to work developing a network to place the children that we rescued. We realized that simply pulling them from hellish conditions would do little to change their lives. Without intervention—putting these children in good homes with schooling and healthcare—they would eventually return to the only life they knew, a life prescribed for them by a culture that disdained Christians as the dregs of society and their children as disposable objects to exercise lust.

Thus, the plan to return to the slave fields was developed, and CRI was born. We were on our way. We had a long, long way to go

Team members and local assets help walk out rescued children.

4

Faisal's Story

A Retelling of the Previous Chapter

FAISAL'S BARE FEET TRIPPED IN THE LOOSE DUST as he ran holding the strings above his head. The owner caught up to him, lifted him in the air, and shook him. With a mocking laugh, he dropped Faisal to the ground, sent a vicious kick to his ribs, and yelled, "You are a foolish boy who does not know how to run. Now do it right or I will beat you."

Blinded by his agony, Faisal scrambled to his feet, brushed off his bare chest, carefully untangled the strings, and ran ten yards to the pole where he hooked them. A machine on the other end braided the strings into rope. Faisal then ran back, grabbed more string, and started all over again, praying he wouldn't trip this time.

Faisal did this twelve hours a day, every day, with no breaks, no food, and little water. He could not afford mistakes. The scars on his back were evidence that the piece of metal rebar the owner wielded was lethal. The owner beat Faisal often—as he did all the boys—usually for no reason.

Faisal had few memories of life before the string factory. His mother had sold him there. The owner taunted him daily—complaining about the price he paid for such a worthless boy that nobody wanted—the price of being a slave forever.

Choking on dust, Faisal saw his chance while the mechanic worked on the rope machine. He darted outside to a large puddle, stooped over, and lapped water like a dog. Another boy, Jacob, ran out to drink as well. Faisal laughed as an exhausted Jacob bent over and fell into the water. They were still children after all. Both boys hurried back, fearing the owner's wrath.

The rope factory was simple in design, diabolical in execution. A large shed was attached to the back of the owner's house. It was a long, narrow roof on poles, surrounded by a brick wall three feet high. It did not provide cover from the wind, but it did shield the workers from the rain. More importantly, it kept the cotton strings dry. It was under this long roof that six or seven barefoot boys ran back and forth all day long, hauling strings to make ropes. Not all of the slaves were children, however. Yusef had been here for several years. His wife was a slave at the brick kiln across the street. They had a young son who was very sick. Faisal tried to help Yusef by holding the toddler when the man went on errands. Most of the time the child was with his mother, but these days she was also sick.

At day's end, Faisal, Jacob, and the other boys were turned out by the owner to beg for food—their only chance for a meal. Sometimes they got handouts, but often they were chased away like vermin by surly business owners.

On this day, as they walked the narrow dirt lanes between brick buildings, Faisal saw a large crowd gathering in a field. Faisal had never seen so many people. The boys stood and watched as buses arrived and the crowd grew.

"What is this?" asked Jacob.

"I don't know," said Faisal. "Maybe a festival?"

Little did they know that this evening would be the start of a whole new life.

"Come! Stand here," a man beckoned to the boys. "Please! Join us."

Faisal glanced around, unsure at first, but something made him trust this man. The other boys followed his lead.

"Stand right up front here," said the man, motioning to the front of a large platform.

There were people as far as they could see. On the platform were some strange-looking men, clearly not from Pakistan. Music filled the air. A man was playing on something they had never seen before. It was beautiful. Faisal couldn't stop staring.

The people around him were dressed in nice clothes. Their skin was smooth, their faces bright. He looked at his own clothes, the torn and dirty rags. He was ashamed. Bending over, he stared at the feet of the man behind him. *Will I ever have shoes like those?*

In time, the music stopped and a Pakistani man with curly hair stepped up to a microphone and introduced himself.

"I am Emanuel. Many of you know me. I grew up among you. I have some special friends here who are going to teach you some profound truths about the love of God."

In excited tones, Emanuel spoke of his friends, strangers who were here to speak to the people. Then a tall, light-skinned man stepped forward and began speaking in a strange language. Faisal, Jacob, and their friends burst out laughing at the stranger's gibberish.

Emanuel translated, telling the people what the stranger was saying.

"My name is Bruce. I am from the United States. I am here to tell you that you can be free. God loves you all. In Jesus Christ, you will find freedom. There is no difference in God's heart between slave or free, man or woman, Pakistani or American. To God, all people are equal, and all are loved."

God? Love? Equal? To hear that God loved them was a concept they did not fully understand.

For an hour, the tall man talked of the wondrous love of a man he called Jesus, a man who was not a man at all but was the Son of God, and that his love was available to everyone.

Then the strangest thing happened. The tall man walked to the edge of the platform, pointed to the boys, and spoke in his funny language. Faisal knew he was in trouble. He cast a furtive glance for a quick exit. The other boys grew restless as well, ready to bolt. But this man was smiling, and not a cruel smile. He was kind, like when a shopkeeper gives them stale bread and maybe a little tea. Emanuel translated for the tall man and asked the boys to come up on the platform. Faisal and Jacob looked at one another, grinned, and scampered up the stairs while the rest of the boys fled for their lives. The tall man leaned down and spoke. Emanuel translated.

"What are your names?"

Staring at their dirty feet, the boys muttered:

"I am Faisal."

"I am Jacob."

"Where are you from?"

The boys answered haltingly.

"We are from the rope factory."

Faisal waited for the curse, the blow, the ground hard against his frail body, the scathing indictment: *Then why are you not at work, you worthless scum?* But it never came. Instead, Emanuel turned and spoke the strange language with the tall man. Turning back to the boys, he said,

"You boys are slaves?"

"Yes."

"This man is Bruce. He is in charge. He is telling me that you are to come to my house for food. Would you like that?"

All Faisal heard was *food*.

It was the biggest house they had ever entered.

"What is happening, Jacob?"

"I don't know. When will they beat us?"

"Maybe they won't."

"Look at this floor. It's so slippery."

"Maybe we should run."

"No, wait. Maybe they will give us some rice. We'll run after that."

Standing in the courtyard, the tall, light-skinned man spoke sharply with Emanuel.

"They're fighting," whispered Jacob.

"Probably over who gets us," whispered Faisal.

The words changed, however, and Emanuel knelt down.

"Faisal and Jacob, I am Emanuel. Would you like to be free from slavery? You could stay here at my house."

"Work here?" asked Faisal.

"Live here," said Emanuel. "Like one of my children. Would you like that?"

"Eat here?"

"Yes," laughed Emanuel. "Eat our food. Grow up here. Never be a slave again. Yes?"

The boys nodded slowly.

"First, you will bathe. And then we will feed you."

Faisal fidgeted. Even though the man spoke Urdu, he was unsure of some of it.

"Please," said Faisal, looking down. "What is *bathe*?"

"Come with me and I'll show you."

While Jacob sat on a chair admiring the tile mosaic decorating the windows, Faisal followed Emanuel to the shower, his eyes fixed on the man's hands. He jumped back when Emanuel made water flow from the pipe in the wall.

"Have you cleaned your body with water like this before?"

"No," yelled Faisal.

"This is soap to clean your body. Rub it on your skin."

Faisal took a tentative step into the stream, laughing as the warm water cascaded over his matted hair and ashen skin. Rivulets of muddy water flowed from his toes.

"It's just like rain!" he said, opening his mouth to taste the clean water.

"Yes, that's right! Rain. Stay there and spread the soap until the foam is white. Then you'll be done."

When the showers were finished, the boys were taken to the dining area. They stared in disbelief.

"A room just for food?" whispered Jacob. "Who is this for?"

"We're probably going to carry their plates for them. Maybe we can eat the scraps. Don't drop them or they'll throw us out!"

To their surprise, they were seated before plates of rice and chicken and other foods they had never seen. Bruce sat across from them, smiling as they ate. Faisal and Jacob ate rapidly, stuffing as much as their mouths could hold, ready to run at a moment's notice. They still couldn't look a man in the eye, but they could risk an upwards glance. Another friend of Bruce's, Robert, smiled at them and babbled in the same strange speech. Emanuel interpreted.

"We love you. You are going to have a good life."

Faisal mulled these strange words in his mind. *We love you. . . .*

Taking their hands in his, Robert then taught them a game called "thumb wrestling." Their fears gave way to hilarity as thumbs danced like cobras.

"Faisal and Jacob," said Emanuel. "Do you want to go to school? Do you want to learn?"

"School?" asked Jacob. "To make bricks?"

"To learn to read and write," said Emanuel. "To study numbers and know what they mean."

Faisal and Jacob knew other children went to school, rough boys who walked past the rope factory, taunting the slave boys as they ran with strings, hitting them when they begged for scraps of food.

"Will they beat us up?" asked Jacob.

"No. This school will be a safe place. You'll go with several other children to a school in a village two hours away. No one will know you once were a slave."

"Will I be in a car? I have always wanted to ride in a car," said Jacob.

"Yes, Jacob," said Emanuel. "We will drive you".

"What about me?" asked Faisal.

"You will stay in my home and go to school near here. You will be my helper."

"Will we make rope?" asked Faisal.

"We will make slaves free," said Emanuel. "I will teach you."

Over the next few days, Faisal and Jacob spent time with Robert, learning more games and simple English like *"please," "thank you,"* and *"I love you."*

At week's end, Jacob left for his new life in another village while Faisal reveled in freedom with Emanuel. It was not without sadness, however.

"Faisal, Bruce and Robert have to leave now. They are going to the United States where they live, a place far away," Emanuel said.

"Do you have to go? When will you come back?" asked Faisal.

"Soon," said Bruce through Emanuel. "And when I do, I expect to see you grown up and strong like Emanuel here, and smart."

Faisal insisted on carrying their luggage to the car, struggling with his malnourished body, pulling the heaviest bags along the ground. He would not be deterred. Even at eight years old, he would show himself strong to these men who were now his friends.

After the goodbyes, the car pulled away. Faisal broke from Emanuel's side and ran along the car until he could no longer keep up, crying out in his new language, "I love you too. I love you!"

His new life of freedom had begun!

Just rescued from horrific abuse, these girls and boys receive gifts and await the journey to their new homes.

5

The Brick Kiln

EVERYONE IN THE VILLAGE KNOWS IT AS THE BRICK KILN—
the gated field where bricks are made. Following a cen-
turies-old tradition, people gather mud and clay, force it
into rectangular-shaped forms, and harden the mixture in
the hellish kiln burning in the center of the yard. The work
is primitive, hot, and deadly. Because labor is cheap—the
price of keeping a person barely alive—the brick kiln is
profitable. The owners grow sleek and fat while the workers suffer, collapse, and are replaced. The people who toil
there are not paid, however. They are owned.

Amir is poor and illiterate. As part of the impoverished
Christian minority in his country, he has no prospects for
education for himself or his children. The survival of his
family depends on the cultural fabric of his community of
slum dwellers, outcasts all. This link is so vital that when
his father dies, Amir knows he has to give him a proper
burial. The scandal of not attending to this obligation could
ostracize him and his family for generations. But where to
turn for the money? He knows of only one place.

Ravier is not tall, but his corpulent presence—wrapped
in starched white robes—commands obedience. The slaves
toil under his sneering gaze, fear the snarl of his voice,

fear the swift arc of the metal baton that never leaves his hand, fear his heavy sandals cracking their ribs, foreheads, limbs—the price for not meeting the day's quota, for fainting in the noonday heat, choking on dust or collapsing when they no longer possess the strength to crawl from the clay pit to the brick forms.

Amir rises the morning after his father dies and wraps himself in his best tunic—a tattered cloth covered in patches. His young wife stares at him, fear in her eyes, tears shimmering in the dim light of their corrugated metal hut.

"It has to be done, Mila," he says.

She nods, lifts their daughter to her breast, and stares at the dirt floor. It is the last thing Amir sees as he ducks through the curtained entrance of the hovel that holds all he loves in life.

Ravier looks past the field of laborers and sees a familiar sight—a gaunt man shuffling toward the gate, head down, hands together in supplication. He smirks. *This will be easy*. With a nod, he orders the guard to let Amir pass.

Four years later, Amir still toils at the brick kiln. It had been a grand funeral. The food, the music, the priests, all was done properly, so said everyone in his community. But the debt has grown from the initial 100, to 300, and now is in the thousands. He can't work fast enough to pay it off. So Ravier makes an offer.

"I'll take 500 off your debt for your wife."

"What about my child?"

"Bring her too. We'll find something for her."

Amir's brother eventually joins them to work off what Ravier said they owed for their father's funeral. Every day, however, they are told they are further behind. And every day, they are ordered to work harder and beaten for their failure.

"Four hundred bricks today? I told you seven hundred. See? You lazy bastards! Why do I even let you stay here? I should turn you over to the police and let you rot in jail!"

Amir has no idea what four hundred is, nor seven hundred, because he can't count. His loyalty to his family has cost him everything. Every day, the scars on his back burn in the midday sun as he hunches over the brick forms. He fights to keep his hands steady as he coughs up blood and black bile and searches for a sip of muddy water from a puddle.

One day, Ravier orders Amir and his brother into the back of a van. They are taken to the basement of the local hospital and given a cherry-flavored drink. When they wake hours later, blood-soaked bandages cover their waists, and stitches mark where a kidney was removed. They burn with fever. An angry guard hauls them outside and into the van. Arriving back at the brick kiln, Ravier bellows: "You were gone all day. You're behind! Now move! FASTER!"

When the confused slaves stumble, Ravier cracks them across the ribs with his rebar stick. Amir shrieks and faints.

It has been years since he has held his wife. When the owners began dragging her into a nearby hut, her screams were more than he could bear, but what could he do? He barely recognizes her anymore. The shy and nervous girl on their wedding night now drags her body through the field of slaves, a skeleton in rags. She never lifts her head, she never smiles, and she no longer screams.

Lately, Ravier has been watching their daughter, calling to her, giving her scraps of bread. She is the only thing

Amir has left in this world. He knows what happens to other children when the owners are through with them. He knows what the night flames of the kiln are for, long after the hardened bricks are slid out to cool. He knows the small bundles wrapped in cloth and the white ash in the morning, covering everything in a layer of pure lies. He knows the silent rage of those who may never rise again—and of those who will.

6

Journey to Freedom

BACK HOME AFTER MY FIRST TRIP TO PAKISTAN, I did as much research as I could but found little information on modern slavery. I posted what I found on social media, and over the next few months, countless people contacted me wanting to know more about labor slavery and sex trafficking. They were horrified that slavery still existed. I was invited to speak many places, but I struggled with being too public. A low profile was necessary to get in *and out* of certain countries.

Several people were eager to go with me on a rescue mission, but I didn't know most of them and I trusted far fewer. One man, John, was a long-term acquaintance who had extensive travel experience.

John was a pastor who had heard about my work in anti-trafficking. With a heart towards missions and a lot of worldwide travel experience, I thought John would make a good addition to the team, although he had some health issues. Slightly overweight, graying hair, and possessing a great personality, John was also wise. I appreciated his sense of humor and maturity. His heart was full of compassion, but I wondered if he could physically handle the trip.

I prayed about him joining and felt peace, so he was added. I knew he would complement my personality well.

John called me a few months prior to the trip and asked if his friend Richard could go. I asked about Richard's qualifications, personality, and ability to handle the trip. He assured me he was a man of integrity and that he could handle the journey. We added Richard to the roster.

I met Richard for the first time at the airport. Tall, with thinning white hair, a short white beard, and life in his eyes—I liked Richard immediately. Richard by profession was a CPA. I was not sure of his physical ability in my first in-person assessment, but hopefully he could handle the stresses of travel and teamwork.

During my travels, a young man named Jody approached me about going on a rescue mission. As I got to know Jody, I was excited to have him join the team. Jody was a two-time taekwondo world champion, well-accustomed to travel, possessed an amazing sense of humor, was an accomplished guitarist and songwriter, and had developed his own combat fighting system. He was the quintessential assistant team leader: alpha, sassy, smart-ass, easy-going, compassionately conservative, and destined for the pastorate. I met him at a men's conference focused on gentleness.

Through phone calls and personal meetings, I prepared this team as best I could. I filled out most of their VISA applications—everything had to be perfect for the Pakistani government officials looking for excuses to deny our visit. The day of departure finally arrived, and our team of four intrepid volunteers headed out to rescue more children.

After arriving in Pakistan and taking a bit of rest at Emanuel's house, we held a two-day leader's conference for 1,200 leaders from around the nation. As inspiring as it was, we were here for more than speaking. Coordinating with Emanuel and his team, we prepared to rescue as many men, women, and children as possible.

A sympathetic government official who knew of our presence advised us to stay in a secure hotel due to increased activity by local religious radicals. His advice was well-timed. As we were settling into our rooms, the hotel staff arrived to move us to new rooms, saying they were installing new carpet in the hallways. *Strange. . . .*

I warned the guys to be careful. These new rooms were likely wired for surveillance. Later that week, a check of the hallways near our original rooms confirmed my suspicions—there were no signs of new carpet. Guarding our words, we crafted a plan. I gave strict orders to the team: "Talk to no one in the hotel. There are secret police everywhere." One guy didn't believe me. Feeling cooped up, he sauntered down to the lobby, took a seat and encountered a very friendly stranger who seemed keenly interested in his presence. In Pakistan, any information is too much information.

A day later, we finally received the call from Emanuel. He and his team had scouted out a brick kiln where slaves were being held in particularly cruel conditions. He knew this brick kiln and its owner from his previous work caring for the slaves. He or his team typically brought them food and water and helped with medical care. With that close contact, Emanuel was able to gather intel on which children or families needed acute care. Still, actually rescuing slaves out of the brick kilns was a foreign concept to him, one he was not entirely comfortable with yet. It was new to us as well, but we were determined to figure it out. It was time to mobilize.

Surrounded by our security team—Pakistani private forces and a police escort—we journeyed to the edge of the city. It seemed strange that we had police escorts, but the Pakistani government did not want anything to happen to foreigners. By now, they knew what we were doing, and in a show of tacit approval, they did not try to stop us. I was approached by the secret police several times, but I always gave the same answer: "We are here to help children, no matter what religion. We want to help children in need." They often followed us, allowing us to become proficient at losing them.

Arriving at the edge of the city, our police escort peeled off, leaving us with our security team to continue to the brick kiln. We never knew what we would encounter in a strange area. Emanuel was great in supplying security—well-trained men with guns—but he did not understand our need for communication. This bothered me a bit, but we were slowly helping him understand operational security and advanced intelligence.

Even though a member of Emanuel's team was sent ahead, there were still unknowns. It was hard to predict a slave owner's reaction. They could be hostile, fearful, shocked, friendly, communicative, or silent. It was silence that concerned us the most.

Forty-five minutes later, with the van's air conditioning straining against the sweltering heat, we arrived at the edge of our first targeted brick kiln. It was easy to find. We closed in on the kiln's signature red brick smokestack spewing filth into the sky, the portrait of evil itself. We piled out of the van, our lungs burning in the dust, and crossed a field to where the slaves worked. Countless rows of bricks were stacked around an area where the workers filled the forms. One slave wheeled mud to another slave, then that slave filled forms as they moved down the row.

The first faces I saw were of a man and his young daughter, who was probably six years old, working on a row of bricks. The innocent child looked up at me and smiled, though sadness was in her eyes. Her dark straight hair was groomed, obviously by a caring parent. She wore a blue jean jacket, a worn blouse, and dirty cotton pants. The father wore an old shirt as well, plus a cross necklace, and worn pants covered in mud from the knees down. They both had mud-caked hands and bare feet coated in the sand in which they knelt. My team stared in unbelief; anger filling their eyes. They were seeing modern-day slaves for the first time. The father and daughter went back to filling a small form with mud, packing it with their hands, wiping away the excess, then turning it over and tapping the top so the formed mud would slide out. Undetected, we moved a little farther into the brickfield.

In the next row were three small girls turning over bricks. Slave owners valued little children (usually ages three to five) for their light weight. They can walk on the drying bricks and turn them over without breaking them. Small children are a commodity in this slave culture. The three girls did not smile nor make eye contact with us; they continued working hard lest they be beaten.

I struggled to contain my emotions. No matter how many times I encountered slaves, I could not get used to it.

It filled me with rage for the perpetrators and compassion for the victims. *Enough of this. Time for action.*

"Emanuel, let's get these people out of here."

"Yes, Dad. We must find the owner first."

Emanuel found the father and mother of the three girls, called them over, and explained that we were going to set them all free. The man, with his head down, lamented that the owner kept adding money to his debt. He owed more than he could ever pay off.

"We will work it out," Emanuel assured the father.

Jody's face said it all. He wanted to work it out with the owner, all right—with interest.

John shook his head in disbelief. "I've been all over the world and I've never seen anything like this."

I gazed at the family. The parent's faces were worn. I could tell life was brutal for them. I gave a cursory glance at the girls, looking for the gold nose piercing that indicated they were the sexual property of the owner. I saw none, although I later found out that this is not always the case. They may still have been abused even though they were not given the nose stud.

The man we had first seen stood near us with his entire family, wondering if they, too, would be rescued. The woman held a newborn. Their worn eyes pleaded with us in a language we understood all too well.

"Dad, this baby will never know life as a slave if we can free them," Emanuel said. "Perhaps we can come back and get them?"

How do we take one family and leave another?

Emanuel listened to the growing chatter among the slaves.

"Dad, the owner is on his way. We need to wait across the road at the building."

We started the long walk back to the road, and a number of slaves followed us. One of the little girls of the family we were rescuing grabbed my hand and looked into my eyes with such melancholy that she captured my heart. Word of our presence was spreading across the brick kiln like a grass fire in hot wind. The children of the families locked hands and walked with us. I was now leading a covey of precious little humans out of this hellhole. *Is this how Moses felt?*

At the van, the family of five climbed into one seat. The children felt the smooth, clean seats and smiled. The man that we first saw had followed, bringing his family too. *Okay, I guess we're taking two families.*

We showed the second family how to fit in the back seat. Now we had four adults, a newborn baby, six girls, two little boys, and an older boy who silently slipped in. We took them all; no questions asked. John stuck his head through the van's open doorway and handed flowers to the mothers.

"For your first day of freedom," he said, beaming. He put his hand on the closest mother's hand. "It's okay. You're never coming back here." He slid the door closed.

Surrounded now by thirty or more slaves, all begging to be rescued, I knew we could not free them today. We simply did not have the resources. As we waited for the owner to arrive, we promised to send the slaves food and clothing.

Suddenly, he appeared in the midst of the crowd. *Safety in numbers?* He was a short, corpulent man dressed in an expensive white robe and sporting a bill-less cap. His head was raised in the manner of men who are accustomed to being obeyed without question. Clearly, he lived well. *Just look at what you can buy with the lives of slaves.*

I had given strict instructions to not open the van doors. I did not want this scum to see the slaves we had secured, nor for them to see him. Even in our care, his visage could evoke fear. This particular owner had a reputation for cruelty. Men and women told me of their spouses being beaten to death. Children were also among his victims, often killed to teach the parents a lesson.

The owner barked something to Emanuel while motioning to the sea of gathered slaves. His face was livid, his glare unassailable as he waited in silence, demanding an answer.

Ringed by our formidable security team, Emanuel answered courteously while I stared down the owner, meeting him rage for rage, my face conveying our conviction that we meant business.

"Tell him we are taking a family," I said, interrupting Emanuel's entreaties.

I did not tell him we had two families. Why should I? They no longer belonged to him.

Emanuel resumed the conversation as I moved closer to the owner. His fierce eyes darted from me to Emanuel, to the security team and back to me, judging my determination, looking for an advantage in this test of wills, and finding none.

We are not leaving empty-handed.

Eventually, the slave owner turned his head, shouted something, and an assistant appeared carrying the record book of debts. Emanuel studied it as slaves around us mumbled among themselves. I assumed they hoped to be freed as well. Even though we could not take them all, we had planted a seed. *This is what freedom looks like. It's worth fighting for.*

"Here are their debt amounts," the owner proclaimed. "If you want to take them, you will have to pay off all they owe."

"How much is their debt?" I asked, looking at the book.

"It's about $900!" said Emanuel.

"They can't even read or write, but you write in the books, you write and write and write in the books," I said through Emanuel. "How can they ever repay you?"

"These people work from generation to generation," said the owner. "They have to pay off the debt they incur. We bought these people and they have to work for us. They got the money; they have to pay it back."

"Why does debt keep increasing?" asked Emanuel. "How does $250 become $500 of never-ending debt over generations? The man who received money from you cannot pay it back."

"The system here is that these slaves can never pay off their debt," I said. "That's the way you have it set up. Come on, Emanuel, let's just take them and go."

"You went on strike against the government," said Emanuel to the owner. "And these people had no food and were dying, yet you gave them no food."

"If there is no work, there is no food," said the owner with a shrug. "Who are you to challenge me? These children have no rights. These Christian people have to serve us. Even though you have support from the government, no one can stop us from working the children. It is legal for us to have the children work. It is between us and the slave. Children have no sense. Our slaves have no right to go to school."

"Yes, they have no rights; they can't go to school," said Emanuel. "They never learn to read, and they don't know that you are cheating them. How much do we need to pay you?"

"You have to pay it all."

"We will NEVER give you all of it."

"Then you have no right to take them."

"Tell him there is a group bringing change to this nation," I said. "And no one will be able to do business like this in the future. On second thought, let's just take the slaves and go. Screw him."

"If you can break this slavery, then go ahead and do it," said the owner. "If you want to take this family, then give me all the money they owe. I bought this family. If you want to rescue them, then give me the money, and you give them a job."

"We want to save their lives," said Emanuel, compassion in his voice. "You are killing them."

"If you want to save their lives, then save them. Go ahead if you have the power from the government. These slave families work for us. We have no boundaries. If they escape, they will be found and punished. If you want to rescue them, you will have to pay for them. Give me the money."

"Cooperate with us," said Emanuel. "We came because we want to rescue the slave families and put the children into schools. This team with me is from the United States.

We are against child labor, and yet in the brickfields, children are working."

"I will not cooperate! All different factories have their own rules. Like God rules over the world, we rule over this brickfield. If you want to rescue these families, pay for them to get out, give them jobs, and take them to the United States."

"You have babies and children. Take mercy on these people and their children."

"No, they are Christians, and they must work for us."

"We are taking these children, one way or another," I said fiercely, counting on the owner's smattering of English language. "Do you understand me, sir? We represent high officials. DO YOU UNDERSTAND?"

"I don't care who you represent. You are costing me money."

"I am very serious," I said. "These people are going with us. I will send government people back here if I have to."

"I don't care."

"Emanuel, let's get out of here before I kill this piece of crap!"

"No, Dad, please don't, or we will all suffer for what you do."

"Here, offer him this and let's leave with the slaves," I said, throwing down a fistful of money—barely anything. "He can follow us if he wants."

Although I hated everything this man stood for, our position was precarious. Depending on the region, especially in areas held by radicals, we had to be careful not to trigger a mass killing of minorities. The radicals were always looking for an excuse to slaughter. This is why we began to exchange money for slaves. It was never much, just a small amount, and we never paid the money ourselves. It is against international law to pay for human life. Our way around this was to give the money to the slaves and have them hand it to the owner. Then, with great fanfare, we would write "DEBT CANCELED" in the debt book with big red Xs next to their names. These were powerful moments in the brick kilns, when those in bondage paid for their release. It affirmed the ex-slaves and humiliated the ex-owners, searing their consciences—if that was even possible.

In this case, however, we did not want this slave owner to see the families, so a representative handed off the small sum of money.

I enjoyed watching the owner choke on his bile. We were taking his commodity, his profit, and in the case of the girls, his lust. Perhaps he planned on taking some slaves to the clinic to sell their kidneys. Organ harvesting was a thriving business in this country. The slaves who lost an organ went back to work, assuming they survived. If they died, the owner would merely go to the slum and buy more. Whatever his plans were for these people, he was pissed and I was pleased. We didn't come to fight. Not when it comes to children. We came to win.

To my great relief, the owner glared at the currency, snatched it up and turned to spit his frustration. We didn't wait for him to get over it. As in any contest of shock and awe, victory has a brief shelf life, and there comes a moment to seize the advantage and leave.

The team and I jumped into the vehicles and sped away, joyous for the slaves we rescued, but heartsick for the ones left standing. Dozens of forlorn faces, haggard and hopeless, stared down the road. I forced myself to focus on the road ahead. *Choose your battles, Bruce. Live to fight again.*

After several miles, we stopped at the modest home Emanuel had turned into a sanctuary for newly rescued slaves. The team and I crowded into the room as the families were seated. I faced these newly emancipated souls and smiled. The team was feeling it too. They just helped free their first slaves. Speaking through an interpreter, one man said he was starving so he borrowed money from the brick kiln, which subsequently led to debt bondage. It would have lasted for several generations had we not intervened.

As food and hot tea were served, the first man we saw with his daughter became overcome with fear and asked to return to the brick kiln. He was born into slavery, and it was all he knew. We assured him that we would set him and his family up with a house and a job. (He was later given a fully furnished fruit stand and educated in business. The family was given a home, and the children were enrolled in school.) You can take the people out of slavery, but it is difficult to take the slavery out of the people. Time and love are key ingredients—and lots of it.

After we ate, John, Jody, and Richard took turns holding the baby. *What is going on in these freed people's minds? One minute a slave, the next minute free and off to a new life.*

Emanuel's team took them to their new lives where volunteers would look out for them. Two local people who had helped Emanuel plan the rescue came to the house to meet with the former slaves. They were a local pastor and his daughter. The daughter was in her twenties and was studying to become a lawyer. She had also gained some notoriety for refusing to wear a head covering like the women around her. For this, she was constantly harassed. We found out later that this father/daughter team was tracked down the day after the rescue and beaten severely. They would live, but they needed time to heal.

They were brave people committed to freedom, and they made my sacrifice nothing in comparison.

7

The Children's Center

PEOPLE OFTEN ASK ME what happens to the children we rescue. How can we ensure that they aren't resold into slavery? The answer is that rescuing these children is more than just freeing them from the slave owners. We sponsor children's centers run by locals, where the children are cared for until they are old enough to be on their own. This includes education, medical attention, and counseling—preparing children for their futures. Here is the story of one such center.

*****

It had been a good day. We had rescued two families from a slave owner infamous for cruelty. As John, Jody, Richard, and I sat, quietly processing the events of the day, Emanuel spoke: "Dad, let me show you what we've done with the money you sent us to care for the children."

I looked at my team. They were ready. With a word and a nod from Emanuel, our caravan was on its way. As we entered the town, however, my instincts went on high alert. Despite being surrounded by Pakistani security—you did not go anywhere in Pakistan without a team of armed security, many of them former Pakistani military—I felt a grave unease. *Think, Bruce! Something is off. What is it?*

"Emanuel, where are we going?"

"You will see, Dad."

"I will see what, Emanuel?"

"Patience, Dad."

We turned into a narrow alley, reached a dead end, and followed the security detail down a path to a modest building, where we entered through its doorway.

Then it happened. Rose petals exploded in the air. We were greeted by a courtyard full of cheering children and adults, jumping and waving—at least 140 people. We were overwhelmed. Teachers led them in song as the children serenaded us. It was glorious, and it went on for several minutes. Amidst the joyful noise and my still racing heart, Emanuel leaned in and spoke somber words in my ear.

"Dad, most of these children are ones we have rescued, but thirty-eight of them still belong to the slave owner. They must work in the brickfields each day."

"What? Emanuel, we cannot let them go back to work. They are just children. We are going to free them."

"How, Dad? How do we rescue so many?"

"We'll find a way. There's always a way."

"I understand, Dad."

Amidst the resounding excitement, Emanuel went to talk with his team. Jody filmed the celebrating children, and John and Richard stepped out of the room for some cooler air. It was a sweltering 120°F in the room.

The couple who oversaw this rescue center, Ayesha and Ahmed, introduced themselves and a conversation ensued. At one point, they mentioned that all 140 children slept where we were standing.

"They all sleep in this little room?" I asked.

"Yes, all of them," Ayesha replied matter-of-factly.

"Right on the cement floor?"

"Of course. Where else would they sleep?"

"We will provide blankets to cover the floor, and we'll make sure they have proper clothing," I said. "Also, how often do these children get fed?" I knew our budget was stretched, but I did not expect the answer I received.

"Perhaps two or three times a week," replied Ahmed. "Today is special. We have rice and chicken arriving soon. Enough for everybody."

"Two or three times? What do they do the rest of the week?"

The silence on their faces spoke volumes. In a quiet voice, Ahmed said, "They beg."

"They beg?"

Freed children . . .still hungry . . .still begging. No!

We had been raising funds for all the work we were doing: rescuing children, building schools, buying food, feeding slaves, providing medical care, and so much more. Clearly, we needed more resources. I immediately posted the need on social media with a link for giving. The money started coming in over the next few days. With adequate funds, we could do significantly more for these children.

Hearing excited voices, I saw the children moving towards the doorway.

"The rice will be ready in ten minutes," Ayesha said. "Now stand back, or they won't be able to get in." The children cheered and cleared a path, expectation all over their faces. Despite the fact that it had been many hours since lunch, I wasn't hungry anymore.

I stepped outside and greeted the security detail covering the doorway. A dirt field pockmarked by tuffs of tall, ugly grass and garbage served as a front yard. Surrounded by decrepit brick buildings, my situational awareness kicked in. I surveyed the area, scanning rooftop to rooftop. Roughly seventy yards away were two radicals staring down at me. I knew them by their trademark headscarves and dark clothes. They were lookouts, keeping an eye on us. Our security guys, each carrying an AK-47, were already aware of their presence and did not seem concerned. I was determined to follow their example.

From down the pathway came the *plod plod plod* of a donkey cart. Door Dash had arrived! Two sets of men lifted large pots using poles slid through the handles. They carried the rice and chicken inside the Children's Center just as the slave owner arrived.

As an owner of multiple brickfields, this owner was somewhat of a big deal among the others. I couldn't imagine why. I saw a small, greasy man with matted hair and garish rings on his fingers. Clothed in traditional garb, everything about him was filthy—from his dirty hair and grimy hands to the robe where he wiped them, to the worn sandals wrapped around his gnarled feet. I turned away to say something to Jody, when I saw a quick motion out of the corner of my eye. Emanuel had slammed the owner against the concrete wall.

"Emanuel? What the—"

The owner screamed, slid to the floor and covered his head with his hands. I whirled around as one of our security guys joined Emanuel in unleashing a tirade of Urdu at the crumpled mass. The crowd of hungry children fell silent, all thoughts of food forgotten.

Hovering over the prostrate wretch, my gentle host looked at me with tears of vengeance: "Dad, he beat two little girls to death. Our girls. Christians!"

Surrounded by the innocent lives that he tortured daily, this repulsive beast had the nerve to show his face in this place! *How could anyone be so brazen?* I stared him down, quivering with murderous intent, then took two steps in his direction. I didn't know where this would end, but I was no longer in control. Fortunately, Richard the Kindhearted reached the slave owner first, knelt down, and offered him water.

Turning to me, he said quietly, "It's the right thing to do."

He was right, of course. I stepped outside, thankful I didn't reach the scum. When I returned clear-headed, Emanuel was in another room negotiating with the slave owner, who was demanding a lot of money to release the remaining thirty-eight children.

"They all have many debts," he insisted.

I moved in closer, my anger cooled to the fine edge of argument.

"Explain to me how any of these children could have debts," I demanded as Emanuel interpreted. "How can a three-year-old owe you money? They're all orphans."

"Their parents had debt," he said arrogantly. "Even though their parents are dead, these children must pay it off. All of it!"

Unfortunately, at this stage in my rescue experience, I was not sure what to do. "Emanuel, we should have him arrested," I said.

"No, Dad, he is friends with the police. They will do nothing. They will not help anyone who is helping slaves."

Emanuel continued in Urdu—mostly likely seeing my lack of fluency as a blessing at this moment—and an agreement was finally reached. We went back to the courtyard and announced to the thirty-eight children that they would not have to work in the brickfields ever again. They were free! But it wasn't enough to hear it from a foreigner—I had to seal their emancipation in a way they could never forget—from the mouth of the devil himself.

I marched the owner into the room so he could tell the children in his own words. "You do not work any-more," he said curtly, then turned and marched off, but not before Emanuel led the children in chanting: "NO MORE BRICKS!" Clapping, they started quietly, growing louder with each chorus as their former tormenter rushed for the exit. They were officially free!

Later, we reported the murder of the girls to the local police and tried to get the owner arrested, but as Emanuel said, the police did nothing. Apparently, murder is legal here. I guess I should have killed him.

After the owner left, we took a group photo with the newly rescued children and promised Aysha and Ahmed blankets and more food. It had been quite the day! First the two families, then a confrontation, and now thirty-eight children had been rescued.

Sometimes, when I closed my eyes, it felt like winning.

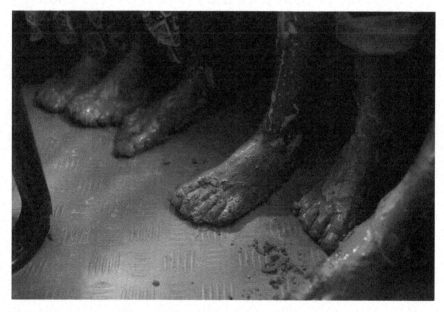

Sitting in the van, children covered in mud are heading to their new homes.

8

Factories of the Enslaved

FLUSH FROM THE PREVIOUS DAY'S SUCCESS of freeing the thirty-eight enslaved children after our rose-petal shower, we stopped at another brick kiln just off the main road. The towering brick smokestack billowed dark smoke, making the brickfield easy to find. Emanuel knew from an earlier conversation that I wanted to interview the slave owner. Trying a kinder, gentler approach, I hoped to broach the subject of enslaving children, and perhaps enlighten this morally bankrupt individual.

Finding the place unsupervised—the norm in this area where owners ruled with impunity—Robert, Jody, John, and I wandered around a bit, observing both children and adult slaves toiling relentlessly until the owner intercepted us. Resplendent in robes of white and gold, he had with him a man easily identifiable as a radical militant. It was the way he dressed, the black edge of his robes, the green turban, and that steel-eyed look of hatred known only to the religiously possessed. Remarkably, he appeared frightened.

Emanuel and I sat on chairs with both men to our right and our security team positioned around us. Emanuel explained to the owner that I was curious about his business. Their self-righteous attitudes betrayed their alarm.

"Where do you sell your bricks?" I asked casually.

"Wherever we want," they replied arrogantly.

I tried a few more conversation starters, all to no avail. It was evident this was not going to be a productive conversation. Possibly feeling outnumbered—four Americans, Emanuel, and our security—the owner and his pet radical jumped to their feet and turned to walk away. I seized the opportunity.

"Emanuel," I said loudly. "I'd like to see the furnace. But before I do, can we get a picture with this fine owner?"

Catching up to the man, and much to his dismay, I stood next to him as Emanuel clicked the camera. The green-turban-wearing radical closed his eyes, possibly thinking this would prevent us from capturing his soul. *A little late to worry about that, Bud.* My courtesy barely masked my contempt. I looked at Jody; his eyes echoed everything I was feeling.

Even though I had been in a dozen brickfields, I had never examined an actual kiln—the brick-hardening furnace at the heart of this blood-stained factory. The dome of a brick kiln is a big mound of dirt supported precariously by a brick skeleton spanning out from the center. Climbing on one of these beasts, you had to be very careful where you stepped; it was easy to break through. Standing atop the furnace, we looked through the vent holes. The coals below glowed white hot. Imagining slaves weary from long days of sweltering heat and toil, we realized that one misstep would cause a collapse of the roof and incinerate a human—a harrowing vision.

Walking down the other side to the main opening of the furnace, we encountered a slave who looked to be in his sixties—ancient by slave standards. Emanuel chatted with him for a little while, then I heard my friend say, "Oh my God."

"What's the matter, Emanuel? What did he say?" I asked.

"Oh my God," he repeated, horror on his face. "Dad, this man is saying that when the children die, they throw the bodies into the furnace."

I stood still, not quite grasping this. When the reality of Emanuel's words pierced my shock, I was homicidal. The rest of the team shared in my growing rage.

"Dad," continued Emanuel. "They won't bury them because they think the bodies of slaves defile their ground."

It was time to go. I couldn't remain there for another minute. The owner and his radical buddy had disappeared, and we did not want to hang around waiting for an ambush, or to commit one ourselves.

My sleep was fitful that night. Distant shooting kept me awake. I never found out what it was, but I could not relax. Overwhelmed by emotion and the atmosphere of oppression, I turned my heart to prayer, felt a sense of relief, and got a few hours of rest. I knew that the only safe place for my mind and emotions was in the presence of God.

The next morning, Richard and John decided to stay at the hotel to rest. Emanuel took Jody and me to the place children were sold into slavery. Driving through the city, we arrived at a tent slum built over a dump. Women and children picked through the garbage for anything valuable—food scraps, metal—whatever they could sell or consume. All eyes were on us as we exited our vehicles fresh from air conditioning, tall and well-fed.

With cameras in hand, we strolled through the garbage-strewn field, encountering an ever-growing group of ragged children. Emanuel explained that this is where the factory owners come to buy children. Their parents are so poor and illiterate, they don't really understand what is happening. Most think they are sending their children off to good jobs and a bright future.

I surveyed the scene, filled with compassion for the people and disgust for the filth. No human should live like this. A small group of children covered in dirt, flies, and soiled clothing attached themselves to us. They smiled and giggled, some shy, others bold. With this group in the background, Jody videoed me talking about how the children will most likely be sold into slavery—hard labor, domestic servitude, or the sex trade—their lives cut short when their frail bodies finally give way to the abuse. After the video had been shot, I looked into the children's eyes. Even though they lived in squalor, there was still a sparkle. It was painful to imagine these beautiful lives being cut short after a life of horror.

"Emanuel, can we just take these children?"

As I spoke, I heard a commotion in the distance. Two men in dark pants and Nike sneakers strapped a terrified boy onto a motorcycle and zoomed off. Emanuel spoke to one of the slum dwellers for an explanation. "Dad, that child was just sold to those men."

"Let's go!" I yelled.

We jumped into our vehicles but could not keep up with the motorcycle because of the rutted roads. I wanted to interrogate these men, find out where they were taking the boy. I wasn't sure what I would have done next, but we could have at least gotten some information.

Having left the slum area, we set out to a rope factory like the one Faisal came from. Stopped on the side of the road, Jody and I drew a lot of attention. Following Emanuel and the security guys, we walked down an alleyway to where ropes were made. It was a small operation with a dozen slave boys running back and forth with fibers that they placed on a hook. The machine at the other end controlled the wrapping process. Just as we arrived, a boy fell, only to be clubbed by the owner with a piece of bamboo. Emboldened by his fury, and by way of introducing our presence, Emanuel walked over to the owner, took the rod and broke it. He then said something I did not understand, but needed no interpretation. It was harsh. For all his gentleness, Emanuel was a force to be reckoned with when confronted with injustice. The boy got up, tears wetting the dust on his face, and continued running back and forth, crying the whole time.

I wanted to run for him, to carry the fibers to the hooks, to take his place while he composed himself. Perhaps he could come back in twenty years and beat the owner with a stick. But there was nothing we could do. We were deep into dangerous territory, lacking our usual (and necessary) ground support. We could have easily dispatched the man and snatched the boy, but the consequences would have been grave for us and the Christian minority in the area. As I was learning, it takes very little to stir up the hornet's nest, and slaughter is a most effective tool.

We drove another quarter mile and stopped at another rope factory. This time we encountered a group of men by the factory; they sat smoking and talking in a circle of wooden chairs. We walked right past them and invaded the factory. The overseer on duty, a disgusting pseudo-man with a sneer and yellow, fiendish eyes, held a three-foot piece of rebar that he used to beat the children. On impulse, I ripped it from his hand. He stared in shock but made no move to retrieve it. We took some video, then demanded to see the owners, who were, as it turned out, the men sitting in the chairs. Once again trying to get them to open up and talk freely, I asked some benign questions

"Tell me about business here."

"You should know," one of them said. "You are from here."

Ah, let the arrogance begin.

"And why do you beat the children?" I asked.

With a raised voice, one of the men answered, "If the children do not work, then we beat them. Only if they do not work."

"Is this the way of your god?" I asked.

An ugly man with a tobacco-stained beard spoke above the murmuring of these fellows. "If this is not the way of God, then you give them food, you give them water. That is why they sell them and we buy them," he said, waving a cigarette through the air with authority.

I was growing tired of these bullshit answers. Diplomacy is a mask that quickly thins.

"Yes, I understand that you buy them, but why can't you take care of the children as your god would require?"

The cigarette man waved again. "We cannot provide them food."

"So the children have to go beg for food?"

"They get food once a day. It is all they deserve."

Their voices grew louder as Emanuel challenged these barbarians, taking over the conversation from my beleaguered interpretation. "You are right. I am one of you. And I know how you operate. I feed those that you starve. I clean those that you soil. And I set free those that you enslave."

One man became so irritated that he squatted on his chair. He looked ready to spring forth and fight. I was hoping he would.

"Why is it like this in this country?" I asked. "Why do you treat children this way?"

"We do not have to answer," came the reply from the ugly bearded man.

"Do you want to see change? Instead of enslaving people, you could hire them and treat them well."

The squatting man replied, "It is good for them to work here. Otherwise, let them go get an education. If not, this is all they are good for."

He knew education for slave children was impossible. So did everyone else. Educate them and there will no longer be slaves to do the work. Disgusted with their cockiness, I pressed them with more questions. The bearded man with the cigarette between his fingers put his hands over his face, tiring of my interrogations.

"Do you give them food and water?" I inquired.

"Yes, sometimes," came the lie through nicotine-stained fingers.

"If you were good businessmen, you'd take better care of the children so they could work well and be healthier."

The bearded man replied with what we have heard time after time. "We could do these things, but why should we care? The government does not care, so why should we?"

I cannot tell you how many times I have heard that phrase. It was time to leave and figure out how to rescue a few of the boys from this accursed factory, if not on this trip, then the next. As our teams often said, "We can't rescue everyone, but everyone we rescue is another death knell to nation-state slavery."

Blankets for Slaves

Nights on a rescue operation are always restless for me. My mind races through all that I experience. It is hard to turn off the images of struggling children—so much suffering, so many abused and tortured people. It is hard on my soul, yet I am not the one in slavery. I have learned to push back the thoughts and trudge on till morning, praying I never grow complacent to the horrors all around me.

Our plans the next day were to visit some leaders and later, visit another brick kiln after dark. The seasons were changing and the nighttime temperatures were falling, bringing further hardship on the slaves. Going from 100°F to 50°F while wearing the same thin, sweat-soaked clothes was brutal.

Arriving at the brickfield after sunset, we slipped out of the cramped car and into the darkness. We drew our flashlights and walked the uneven ground to the brick-forming area. Faint sounds of whimpering permeated the darkness. I shined the flashlight on a dozen shivering children turning bricks. None of us could believe what we saw. In total darkness, these children, shaking and crying, wearing nothing but thin clothes, were made to turn over the cooling bricks. They worked all day in the hot sun, and as darkness crept in, were forced to work in plunging temperatures. I photographed the scene, the images forever seared into my psyche.

Emanuel, Jody and I looked at each other. We knew we had to do something for these precious children. Driving back to the city, we discussed how to help them. Rescue was not possible there, as the slave master was too powerful and well-connected politically, yet we had to do something.

Back in our rooms, I went on social media and requested donations for blankets. Slaves have very few possessions; we wanted to give them thick blankets and proper clothing. Within a few days, enough money came in for two hundred blankets. Driving back to the brick kiln, every head in the place raised up to see who was there. We started pulling out dozens of heavy multi-colored blankets. Slaves came from all over the fields. We passed out the blankets as quickly as we could; soon there were none. The slaves' eyes told us they were thankful. We knew they'd be warm, at least this evening. Hopefully, the slave owner would not steal the blankets. The cruelty of slave owners is beyond my understanding. We now raise money every year just for blankets.

The Heart of Hell

The following day, we left for a city controlled by radical militants. It was our last trip before leaving for home. It had been my desire to meet with government representatives to

discuss the plight of children. Emanuel, through a government connection, arranged for us to meet one of the highest
political figures in the nation.

In the early morning hours, we launched out for the
eight-hour drive to a northern city. With beautiful vistas
along the way, it was hard to imagine the rebel camps and
radical training centers hidden deep in those mountains.
At different roadside junctures on the drive, radicals were
amassed in numbers. We stayed in the car, our windows
darkened by mesh shades, while our indigenous team
members got beverages and used the facilities. We westerners took our toilet breaks in more secure areas. As we
rose in altitude, the scenery grew more spectacular, valleys
and mountains filled with beautiful foliage.

Entering our destination city, it was apparent that it
was controlled by radicals. The atmosphere felt strangely
different; oppression as thick as smoke. The colors everywhere were muted to black and white. The people, with
heads lowered, walked a fine line between submission and
slaughter.

Just to get into the hotel for the meeting, we had to go
through four levels of security. I cannot elaborate on the
meetings with the high-level government officials, but they
were very close to the top. At one point in the hotel restaurant, this high-ranking official (who was over this entire
territory) told me that I was sitting in the same spot that
an infamous terrorist once sat to plan some of the world's
worst events. We had certainly gone deep into enemy
territory.

As I pondered this nugget of infamy, I looked out the
back window to see several rebel warriors coming in

through a private entrance. I leaned toward Jody, the most well-trained of my team, and whispered, "Be on high alert."

The rebels looked fierce. In a show of force, they came our way and sat at a table a few feet away. I motioned to John and Richard, the pastors of the team, to avoid making eye contact. I turned my chair slightly to keep the radicals in my peripheral vision. At one point, I slipped up and made eye contact with the fiercest, scariest-looking guy I had ever seen. I gave him a smile, one of those smiles that said: *"I am not afraid of you."* I knew these guys hated us and would kill us if given the opportunity. The high-ranking official later told me they were an extremely feared group, responsible for many horrific events.

We had come to this stronghold to discuss the plight of children and perhaps establish a rescue operation in this city. Many of the Christian children here were taken for slavery or sold into the international trafficking markets. Some were used for suicide missions.

I did not sleep well in the hotel that night; my soul was burdened. I have never been able to even slightly comprehend the mentality that agrees with enslaving others, especially children. I was also very aware that we were in an immensely dangerous area. Jody slept fitfully as well.

The next day, we traveled to meet a group of Christians at a secret location. They held church there and met for other reasons. I hoped to get an interview or at least gather some information on why these poor souls would sell their own children. As we drove along, we saw several bombed-out buildings. We were told the rebels had recently kidnapped a very important person there. When I asked for details, the locals simply shrugged. Apparently, this was too commonplace to worry about. We turned down some narrow alleys, drove across a dirt paddock, and parked by a group of people who did not look at all pleased to see us. They were dressed differently than the Pakistanis. Emanuel said they were Afghanis. I think they were upset at seeing foreigners here—strangers usually spelled trouble.

Exiting the car, I saw that the field was surrounded by buildings, some several stories tall. I watched the eyes of our security as they surveyed the rooftops. Jody and I followed their gaze as we were escorted down an even narrower alleyway into a small meeting hall where fifty people were gathered. After some formalities and a few songs, Emanuel and John addressed the group, then I asked some questions.

"First of all, thank you for having us here. I know that life is tough for you. I would like to ask a few questions. I would like to know how many of you have sold a child."

A dozen hands went up.

"Why did you sell your child?"

Emanuel was translating the questions and waiting for the answers. He leaned closer to one woman who was talking quietly.

"Dad, she says they are all so poor that they cannot keep all of their children."

Emanuel explained that they had zero education and no birth control, so they had many children.

"Emanuel, please ask them if they know what happens to their children once they sell them."

"I do not know," said a woman in the back.

"I think my child has a job somewhere," said another.

The reality was clear. They did it to survive, not knowing or perhaps denying what really happens. I am sure that after centuries of slavery in these nations, the truth is known, but knowing and being able to do something is vastly different.

Leaving the building, we encountered a group of people in the field who wanted to talk to us. We had no clue why, but Emanuel became agitated. I looked around.

"What's wrong, Emanuel?"

"Dad, these are also Afghanis."

"What do they want with us?"

"That's what doesn't make sense, Dad."

As we chatted with this group, one of the security men noticed several flags being raised on rooftops nearby, signaling a warning or possibly an attack. Suddenly, it all made sense.

"We need to leave immediately," Emanuel said.

I realized the danger we were in. The group talking with us was trying to stall us. A few minutes more and we would be ambushed. We bolted.

Later that evening, we embarked on the eight-hour journey to the airport and then on to the United States. We freed seventy-six slaves on this trip under difficult conditions, got them into new homes under the care of local volunteers, and knew they would be schooled and taught job skills. We had stared into the eyes of Satan himself without flinching. Yet I saw a greater adversary than I had the ability to defeat. Teamed with pastors equipped with humanitarian chutzpah would get us only so far. My mind was a tempest for the multitudes waiting for their deliverance. We had struck a blow against institutional slavery, exploiting its vulnerabilities of overconfidence and arrogance. Now it was time to probe deeper, testing the security of fortifications once thought unassailable. For that, I would need to up our game. I needed seasoned operators, men and women with the guts to change what any sane person would flee; warriors with hearts aflame for the freedom of oppressed children. But where to find these people?

Did I say I don't sleep well on rescue trips? I don't sleep any better at home.

9

Shaimah's Survival

SHAIMAH SLUMPS OVER THE BRICK FORMS AND WEEPS. Every breath brings searing pain through her frail body. In a fit of rage, her master beat her in the ribs with a metal rod because she was sick and could not keep up with the others. Shaimah's chest now burns as she struggles to fill brick forms with mud. She tries to keep moving down the row, but the pain is unbearable. She soiled herself when he attacked her, but she knows she has to keep working. Blood seeps through her thin clothing, mingles with excrement, and streaks down her legs. Flies cover her wounds; she doesn't have the strength to swat them.

The slave owner walks back to the little covered porch where he presides over his kingdom. Mahnoor is a vile, sadistic man. He brags to the slaves about all his money, and boasts of the young girls in his possession. Mahnoor lives in a big home in the nearby city. He spends every day sitting under the covered porch, making sure his slaves toil endlessly to make him even more wealthy. Not content to destroy their bodies, he waits for Shaimah's daughter to turn twelve so he can add her to his girls.

Pain shoots through Shaimah's ribs with every breath, but she knows she must get through the day. The rising sun bears down on the slaves; it is the hot season and nothing moves of its own volition. As Shaimah works down a brick row, she gets close to a small pond. Desperate with thirst, she crawls through the mud and frantically laps muddy water from her cupped hands, fearful that Mahnoor will see her. The brown water tastes so good, but the pain makes it difficult to swallow.

After several gulps, she soaks her hijab, wraps it around her head, then rinses the stain of the beating from her pants. Keeping low, she crawls back to the brick forms and resumes her labor. A young boy, Ayamin, pushes wheelbarrows of mud toward her. There is no end to her labor, starting at dawn and ending deep into the night.

Shaimah was born into slavery. Her parents were slaves. They were bought and sold twice in her lifetime. Her father was eventually beaten to death by another owner. She does not know exactly how old she is, but she knows she is in her thirties. Shaimah knows very little of the outside world. She dreams of a mobile phone to contact relatives. Maybe someday if she was free, she could have her own house.

As evening approaches, Shaimah wears out from the intense burning in her side. There is no medical care or medicine available for her or her family. Tonight, she will use some herbs common among the slaves, but they may not help. Shaimah has had two handfuls of rice today, and her water source is the same pond used for making bricks, the same place that water buffalo drink from as they wander through, the same water that provided a shred of dignity when the stench of her punishment filled the air. In the fading sunlight, she sees her oldest daughter, Alishba, pulling her infant on a blanket as she works the row, forming brick after brick. Shaimah wonders how long Alishba's baby will live. Alishba has been raped many times by the master.

Darkness brings the unrelenting mosquitoes. Miserable and covered in bites, Shaimah covers herself as best as she can, but the mosquitoes still find a way. She can't count the times she and her family have had malaria or dengue fever, but when it happens, they suffer badly—forced to work or endure life-threatening beatings for not working.

Death is common in the slave fields. Shaimah has no education and does not understand how slaves fuel her nation's economy. She only knows that when a slave dies, they are replaced with another that magically appears in the fields. She does not realize that the owner buys and trades slaves through a friend, or that these come mostly from Christian slums—the lowest of the low. She tries to comprehend this system, but she only knows what she has been taught by the slave owners: Christians were created by God to be slaves.

At night, Shaimah, her husband Rizwan, and their five children cram into a small brick hovel under a rusted metal roof. She and her three oldest children each own one set of clothes that she carefully washes weekly and tries to make last. The two youngest have nothing but torn pants.

Shaimah prays nightly to be delivered from slavery, as she has for years. Still, she believes that her prayers will be answered and that she will die free.

Sunrise comes and Shaimah faces another day. She makes the hundred-yard walk back to the brick kiln, knowing the master will come and brutalize her if she doesn't arrive. Without much sleep and in severe pain, Shaimah rubs the herbs on her side and moves slowly along the brick rows. Rizwan toils to supplement her quota, but he is exhausted too. He can't confront the master; he is owned, a mere possession, worse than a dog. To challenge the owner is to be beaten, possibly to death. Rizwan has carried many bodies to the kiln. Like Shaimah, his daily prayer is for freedom.

At midday, the master walks over to another family, grabs their fourteen-year-old daughter, and leads her away. She screams and fights, then goes limp as he drags her to the compound. Several hours later, she walks back in silence, her head down, her clothing disheveled, and resumes ferrying mud for the workers. Although Shaimah has seen this countless times, her rage never diminishes. *You can force us to work for you, but do you have to rape us?*

She knows she is powerless. There is nothing for her to do but keep her head down and work. Her fingers are bent from years of working the brick forms, but she doesn't know that's why. As she toils, she hears Rizwan singing a Christian song as he works, and she finds that comforting. She likes it when he sings. She hopes Pastor Joel will visit. He is a Pakistani Christian who tells stories of the Bible to the slaves as they work. He is kind and gentle, serious without being grim. He is not afraid of the master. Shaimah is glad. He offers so much kindness, and he never stops coming even though he is often beaten by the master and his men.

Several rows over is another family. Rimsha is the mother of eight children. Her husband, Fazeel, was beaten to death by the master a year ago. Rimsha's son was sold to the agricultural farm next to the brick kiln. He died when the owner threw him into a grain chopper because he was very sick and could not work. Two of her daughters were sold to men. She has no idea where they are now or if she will ever see them again. Rimsha's other five children work with her. The youngest is three years old.

Shaimah tries a shallow breath through the pain. Looking past Rimsha, she sees several cars pulling into the brickfield. Sick with fear, her mind screams. *Will Alishba be sold today?*

But the cars drive past the owner's compound and continue towards the brick rows, turning down a row just behind her. She freezes. To her surprise, Pastor Joel bounds from the car. In the second car, men with guns quickly step out and set up a security perimeter around the slaves.

"What is happening?" yells a frightened Alishba.

"Quiet!" Shaimah replies. She knows something is up, and if Pastor Joel is involved, it's something good.

Now men, the likes of which she has never seen, are exiting the car, huge men with light skin and strange clothing. *Who are they?* If it were not for Pastor Joel's presence, she would run.

Pastor Joel walks over to some slaves. Soon all the slaves stand up to see what's happening. Shaimah is confused, but as Pastor Joel talks, the strange men walk toward her, many holding small boxes with glass eyes. They point these at her and her family

One man in the group is like her—though he has lighter skin. He approaches and speaks to her in native Urdu.

"What is your name?"

"Shaimah, Sir. I am Shaimah."

She does not make eye contact; he is a man.

"My name is Emanuel. I have brought these people with me to free you and your family."

"What does that mean?" asks Shaimah cautiously.

"We are taking you and your family and many others from here to give you freedom and a new life."

"I do not understand. I am owned by the master."

Shaimah glances upward as Emanuel puts his hand on her shoulder. Any other day, this touch would mean brutality. Today is different.

"We are here to free you from slavery, Shaimah."

A light breaks through her confusion. *These men are here to answer our prayers!*

"Come everyone! Quickly!" Shaimah cries to her family.

The strange men gather around them. One speaks to her but it doesn't make sense. Emanuel explains that this man, Bruce, has come a long way to rescue her, but they must hurry.

"Quickly, Shaimah," says Emanuel. "Gather your family and follow me."

Shaimah shudders when she sees the master exploding out of the compound. He is enraged, waving his metal rod and screaming at the slaves to get back to work. Without thinking, she turns to the brick forms, but Emanuel gently guides her to her feet and bids her to come with him. Shaimah is torn. She wants so badly to be free, but what is freedom when the master owns her?

Emanuel and Bruce engage the master, who lowers his metal rods and glares at them.

"We are taking many families from you," she hears Emanuel say after Bruce talks in a strange language. "Slavery is wrong. It's against the law."

Shaimah wonders what the word *law means*.

A growing crowd of slaves surrounds the master and the men. The master is waving his arms, yelling at Emanuel. "See what you have started? Now they won't work and they will have to be beaten. You will not take them. They belong to me."

Shaimah is startled when Bruce closes in on the master, stares at him, and speaks in the language she doesn't understand.

"You cannot own people," she hears Emanuel say. "We are taking these Christians to a new life."

"No! They owe me money. I will show you."

The master snaps at his assistant: "Go get the book."

Bruce fires back. "I don't care what your book says. Your numbers lie. We are taking these people."

Her heart erupting, Shaimah turns away and prays to God for these men, for her family, for freedom. Emanuel tells the slaves that he and these men are here to take them to freedom. "You and your children will live in houses. They will go to school. You will have plenty of food."

The master yells, "They are lying. They will hurt you. They want to steal you and take you apart in their hospitals. I can protect you."

Bruce's face is red. He speaks sternly to the master. Shaimah fears the master will beat him, but she sees something in the master's eyes that she has never seen before: *fear.*

Emanuel tells the master what Bruce is saying.

"See these cameras?" The men held up the one-eyed boxes. "We are filming this. It is illegal to force children to work. It is illegal to buy and sell slaves. We are showing this to the world. You will go to jail. Your slaves will return and kill you in your sleep. Is that what you want?"

The master puffs out his chest but no words come from his mouth. Shaimah now understands what the strange devices in the men's hands are for.

The slaves murmur among themselves. "Who are these people? Where are they from?"

Emanuel speaks to the crowd. "You will be taken to a new life."

A few women brave a smile, but the men look confused. Slavery is all they know. "What is *a* new life? What does that mean?" asks one man, bewildered.

One of the men in black with a gun whispers something to Emanuel.

"We must leave now," cries Emanuel to the slaves. "NOW!"

In an instant, forty-five slaves rush to the van. The men with guns get the five families in first, but many more press in and the van doors cannot be closed. Shaimah and her family are pressed into the back.

"Where are we going?" she asks, suffocating but hopeful. No one answers.

Pastor Joel yells into the van. "Is Shaimah in here?"

"Yes, yes. In the back," she hollers.

Pastor Joel asks about other families. All are accounted for.

"Okay, you will all be safe. We are taking you to a place where you will eat good food and have a home. You will be safe."

"What about our pots and blankets?" asks one woman.

"It's okay," Pastor Joel says with a smile. "We will give you new pots and blankets for your new life."

The van pulls out and bounces along the rough road. So many people are piled around Shaimah that it's hard for her to breathe. The needle-like pain in her side screams with every jolt, but nothing can wipe the smile from her face. She clutches her granddaughter to keep her from being crushed. Others talk of the sites along the road, but Shaimah can't see out the windows. The excitement builds the farther they get from the master's brick kiln. One man breaks into song, an old ballad about freedom. Others join in as the van driver confirms that this is indeed a drive to freedom. An old man makes up a song about Emanuel being Moses, and how the Lord sent strange, light-skinned men to carry them across the Red Sea.

Every pothole is agonizing, but Shaimah holds her granddaughter and whispers in her ear. Tonight, they will share a meal and later, a clean bed—the first they have ever known.

God has answered Shaimah's prayers.

Catch Dog sprays a hose as a rescued girl washes off the mud.

10

The Liberandum Directive

2011—The Third Rescue

Liberandum (Latin) – An inflection of liberandus,[6] meaning to be freed, liberated, released, delivered, absolved, acquitted.[7]

*****

"DAD, COME DOWN HERE. QUICK!"

I opened my bedroom door. The yell from the stairway came again.

"Dad, hurry . . .please!"

Recognizing Emanuel's voice, I slipped on my shoes and sped down the spiral stairs. It was my third visit to Pakistan, and I had taken refuge in my room for some alone time after a heart-wrenching morning in the slave fields trying to rescue children.

Had he been beaten again?

---

[6] "Liberandum Definition", accessed 23 September 2022, https://www.wordsense.eu/liberandum/.

[7] "Liberandus Definition", accessed 23 September 2022, https://www.wordsense.eu/liberandus/#Latin.

I sprinted down the hall, turned a corner, and saw Emanuel with the other members of my team standing beside some locals whose gaunt faces and tattered rags could only mean one thing.

"Dad," pleaded Emanuel. "These slaves have come for help. This is their son."

He motioned toward a quivering boy who was about twelve years old.

"Dad, this boy has been burned with acid by the slave owners."

My eyes flooded as I gently approached the boy. Obviously wracked with pain, he lifted his head to reveal the wounds on the side of his face, down his neck, his chest, and most of his leg. Red exposed flesh was on his face, and the infection was evident. I struggled to quell my rage.

"What's your name, son?" I asked quietly.

Emanuel translated my question, and the boy murmured, "Amir."

Tears rolled down his weathered cheeks as he struggled to meet my eyes. It is common for slaves to respond to kindness with a mixture of hope and fear. Clearly, he and his family had been abused for years.

Eric—one of my team members, a military veteran with medical experience—offered to clean and dress the wounds. Eric was tough as nails, an MMA fighter, highly trained, brave, detail-oriented, and extremely passionate about saving children. He understood team dynamics and excelled as a leader. He had a soft side to him that made him a deliberate speaker, careful of others' feelings. When it came to the plight of Pakistan's slaves, Eric's compassion flowed easily into tears. As Eric worked with this precious boy, Emanuel explained what happened.

"Amir was working in the brickfields with his family. They are slaves. His father got sick and could not work, so Amir had to make up for what was lacking. One of the brick kiln's owners got drunk, and when he returned to the fields, he saw that Amir had not fulfilled his quota. In a fit of rage, he threw acid all over the boy's face and side. Amir has not been to the doctor, and now the wounds are infected. His mother heard there was someone helping the slaves, and they walked all the way here, many miles, to get help."

The mother's forlorn look moved my soul. Her face was aged, a scar across her chin, her hair dyed with some natural red substance common to the poorest of this nation. She was dressed in a light-colored shirt and loose cotton pants, both stained with red dirt. She looked weak and defeated.

Emanuel talked with the father and interpreted their story of suffering. It was the typical narrative of indebted slavery—a small loan grew into a lifetime of debt. As the father spoke, he lowered his head, a result of being beaten most of his life. Hearing about their painful lives, the rage I had been suppressing erupted.

"Emanuel, this family cannot go back. As far as I am concerned, from this moment forward, they are free."

"Dad, what do you want me to do?" Emanuel said nervously. "Perhaps the owners should come here, and we will make them promise to never harm these people again."

"No. I am not letting this family go back," I said.

"They look hungry, Dad. We will feed them and then we'll talk some more."

As Emanuel's wife prepared a meal, Emanuel explained to the family that they were free. They never had to touch another brick again. A slight smile revealed itself on the father's face, but the mother broke into a full grin. After they ate, we gave them the funds to take their boy to the hospital for medicine and extensive care. Emanuel provided a driver and the family was taken to a clinic. However, this situation was far from over in my mind.

"Emanuel, I want to meet the men who think it's acceptable to burn a child with acid. We're going to confront these scum—NOW!"

"No, we cannot go right now, Dad!" pleaded Emanuel. "It's not the right time. But we will. . .soon. The family will go back and then we can obtain their release."

My frustration exploded.

"Send them back to the owners? Are you crazy? They'll just abuse them more. Let the family stay here after the hospital and we'll get them a place to live. I'll find the funds. We have to—"

"Dad, I understand," Emanuel interrupted in a tone reserved for anger. "But please remember, this is my country. We will rescue this family, and many more. You have inspired me. Before you came, I only thought of comforting slaves. You brought us a message of freedom. But we are partners. You have to listen to me."

Emanuel's plaintive expression reminded me that I had much to learn about his culture, its legal system, and its thought processes. He knew how things worked here. At times, it seemed fear-based to me, but he was right. (He was usually right.) We were a team. I reached deep down inside for a calm I often dispossessed in my drive to effect change. *Think, Bruce. Emanuel is a champion of his peo-ple. What is his logic here?*

In time, I grew to appreciate how dangerous it was for Emanuel, as a Christian in this country, to do the things he did. He was in the minority; persecution was a norm for Christians. To challenge the system, even in a small way, was rare and often fatal. There were no human rights for minorities. No freedom of speech or the right to a fair and speedy trial. If you were fortunate, you got a quick death.

So, I waited while Emanuel prepared. The next day, Emanuel, my team from the US, and I arrived at the brick kiln, along with our usual cadre of Pakistani security guards arranged for by Emanuel—four Pakistani comman-dos armed to the teeth with AK-47s, pistols, knives, and attitude. My team included Jody, Eric, and our videogra-pher, Aaron.

Aaron was a hometown boy, thirty years old and single, a committed Christian who had never been overseas. He was not a seasoned traveler and had no military training whatsoever. Slightly overweight, average build, and tall, his extreme intelligence meant he could figure out any-thing. It was his talent as an experienced videographer, however, that made him the perfect component for our team. The video camera, it turned out, was indeed mightier than the sword, as Shaimah had witnessed.

Our strategy was simple: Make the owner think we were filming a story for the made-up international news outlet BNN (Bruce's News Network). For all their bluff and bluster, most slave owners were easily intimidated. It's one thing to inflict violence against impoverished children and minority-class adults. Quite another thing to stand up to men and women who knew their place in society and humanity. Slave owners were just bullies.

The owners we were now confronting on a regular basis were ruthless thugs, but they were cowards at heart. Confronted with honest hearts burning with righteous zeal, the brutality of these merchants of malfeasance crumbled.

Also aiding in our efforts were various elements of the Pakistan government. Through Emanuel and his contacts, I have met many members of the Pakistan government and most seemed like good people. Several wanted to eliminate slavery. The slave owners knew this, so they kept a low profile. We hoped the shame of publicity would pressure them to relinquish the slave family in question and possibly change their ways for good.

Finally, we had the element of uncertainty. The world beyond Pakistan is unknown to many of these provincial slavers. We came from another land, another world, immune to their lies and intimidation. They did not know how to deal with us.

Only one of the two owners was at the brick kiln when we arrived. I recognized him from the last time we rescued children from this place. Speaking through Emanuel, I confronted him about Amir.

"Why would you torture a little boy with acid?"

The man answered haughtily, his chest puffed, his chin resolute—the picture of a firm man of action. Yet his fetid breath told me otherwise. With as much as he was panting, he was terrified. *Maybe he's got some good sense after all.*

"Dad, he says the other owner did this, not him," said Emanuel.

"You're lying," I said directly to the owner, my eyes boring into the pathetic portals of his soul.

We continued to pressure him, dogging him with questions that he evaded with a growing stammer. He shuddered each time our security detail shifted its weight. The clacking of weapons ammo was enough to send fear into anyone's spine. This piece of human waste had no spine left.

Breaking down, he became overwhelmed, refused to answer any more questions, and staggered away. I wanted to pursue him. Emanuel, my soul-linked partner, whispered to give him space. Eric followed him at a distance and saw him using a cell phone behind a large stack of bricks.

That's it. He's calling for help. We're getting to him. Good.

When the owner returned, he was sweating profusely. A few minutes later, two guys pulled up on a motorbike. Eyeing Aaron's video camera, our security detail and our no-nonsense expressions, they parked between piles of bricks and called out to the owner. A brief conversation in Urdu ensued.

"Emanuel, are they reinforcements?"

"No. At least . . .I don't think so."

Sensing our opportunity slipping away, I called the owner over and delivered an ultimatum.

"Tell this piece of crap we are taking this family. Their debt is canceled. And if he or anyone else ever hurts a child again, we will be back. And we will take our revenge."

I knew he didn't speak English, at least not well enough to understand every word, but he got the message. Delivery, as they say, is everything.

We rounded up Amir's family and one other family that looked severely abused, and loaded them into three-wheeled rickshaws (a form of taxi in Pakistan) that we hired on the spot. The owner looked resigned and feigned the appearance of superiority, but we knew he was incensed. As Emanuel explained to me often, victories like this don't happen often against the ruling class in Pakistan. Our advantage was that this was a small kiln with less ability to fight back. We, as foreigners, represented international pressure—something that criminals wanted to avoid at all costs.

Before we left, I looked into the rickshaws to make sure everyone was comfortable. The families looked bewildered but excited. I spoke to the children, knowing they would understand even though they had no English.

"You are going on a great new adventure! You are safe. You are free."

They had no clue what freedom was or how their lives were about to change. For all I knew, they were excited to ride in a rickshaw. But that was okay. They were children; let them be such. Their smiles spoke volumes.

Arriving at Emanuel's home, I was ready to toast our success. But Emanuel knew it wasn't over. Later that day, he made arrangements for both of the owners to come to his house to discuss the terms of the surrender of their human possessions. For the second time in as many days, I thought my partner had lost his mind. *Never interrupt your enemy when he is making a mistake.*

"Why would they even come, Emanuel?"

"Dad, the owners are greedy. They have lost their pride. They will come thinking it's a chance to get some of their reputation back, and perhaps an understanding that we'll leave them alone after this. Perhaps they'll be looking for a payoff on the money the slaves owed. Ours is a country of cooperation, Dad. Even among the slave owners."

"But we're not going to give them anything, right?"

"No Dad. They poured acid on this boy. There is no saving face for Amir. There will be no saving face for the owners. That is enough to free Amir and his family."

"Good, because I have something else in mind," I said, flexing my fists.

When they arrived, these enslavers of humans were escorted to my room, a power move I read in a motivational magazine somewhere. *Always meet the enemy on your turf.* I was determined to make these men pay, even if the currency was whatever shred of self-respect they still possessed. As they entered, they saw Amir standing beside me, his face bandaged, arrayed in clean clothes. Their eyes grew as big as saucers.

"Emanuel, tell these vermin that because of what they did to this young man—burned him with acid—they have lost two families and their profit."

The owners avoided eye contact with me as Emanuel translated. They shifted uneasily.

"Now, tell them to apologize to Amir."

"Dad! That is not done here," exclaimed a shocked Emanuel. "They will not apologize to a slave, especially a Christian."

"No," I said calmly, my voice growing stronger with every word. "They will—or there will be a price to pay. It is outrageous that they would torture anyone like this. Tell them they need to ask for forgiveness from the boy. Do it!"

A shaken Emanuel translated my orders. The owners couldn't understand my words, but the tone of my voice conveyed a deadly intent. Both men shuffled their sandaled feet, shifted their gaze to a place on the wall behind us, and uttered something contrite to the boy at my side. Their jarred nerves were evident in their voices. One owner looked ready to wet himself.

"Okay, Dad, they have apologized," said Emanuel quickly. "I think this is the first time a slave owner has ever apologized to a slave boy in this nation. We are finished now, right?"

I was nearly satisfied. *Nearly.*

As my eyes burned through theirs and into the back of their skulls, I said: "Tell these men they can go, but if they ever harm a child again, I will find out and I will be back. And it will not be good for them!"

"Okay, Dad. Okay. Let's get them—."

"Say it, Emanuel. And don't mince words."

I knew their proffered humility was futile since the abuse of slaves was ingrained in the culture. But knowing we had the will to remove their resources and impact their profits hopefully made an impression on them. The men murmured to each other and shuffled out of my presence with their heads down, no doubt assuring each other of their resolve to put this humiliation behind them and take their revenge on this meddlesome foreigner. *That's fine, guys. Have your bravado. We have your slaves. And we know where there are more.*

After they left, we went downstairs to let Amir's family know they were free.

"No more bricks!" we said to them. They picked up the chant. "NO MORE BRICKS!"

We gave them funds to take Amir back to the hospital for more medicine and extensive care, and we assigned members of Emanuel's team to look after them as they acclimated back into the community.

Over the next few years, we returned often to that brick kiln to rescue slaves. Eventually, the pressure became so great that the owners could not remain operational. They went out of business and lost everything, while hundreds of freed slaves regained their freedom.

A slave girl working in the mud pits does not know she
is about to be rescued.

11

Winds of Change

MOUNTING A RESCUE OPERATION with five team members was a new challenge. I liked to travel light to keep our profile low. But operations were also becoming more complex as we targeted greater challenges. Once in Pakistan, Robert, Aaron, Joel, Jody, Eric, and I settled into our accommodation.

Robert was the pastor from our previous visits. He wasn't much with self-defense, but he was valiant of heart and we needed him for the aftercare of rescued slaves—and I needed him to keep me from the edge of violence.

Aaron was also from my previous trip, an outstanding hand in all things electronic. He was our videographer, and he had a knack for being exactly where we needed him without us having to say a word.

Joel was a friend of Aaron's and his opposite in many ways. A dominating figure at six foot one, with a furious white beard, Joel was an accomplished tattoo artist whose skills were displayed in abundance. I liked Joel's independent streak, but saw that he struggled to be a team player. He excelled at photography, and we made sure his function matched his skill set.

Eric was a friend of Jody's; both men were highly trained, fierce in self-defense, and consumed with desire to save these children.

After a brief sleep, we met with Emanuel to learn the plan for the coming days. We were holding a leadership conference where I planned to address the expected crowd of 1,100 on the mandate to rescue children and stop the abuse of women. Given the widespread acceptance of both practices in Pakistan, speaking boldly to an audience was one thing, but knowing that government officials and secret police were in the audience was another matter. *Damn the torpedoes. Full speed ahead!*

Truth is truth, and if I didn't remain authentic each time I did a conference, I could miss the chance to change lives and possibly save them. I frequently angered dangerous people, and certainly, speaking out about women having the same rights as men would only make things worse. But I refused to be intimidated. I spoke the truth. Indeed, truth will always speak. *Torpedoes be damned.*

The conference was held in a beautiful building near a radical stronghold. Several levels of protection had been set up with police and our private security. We had to ensure that weapons could not be slipped into the building. Participants passed through a metal detector before entering the building, but the building staff did not check each other, so we kept an eye on everyone. This type of meeting was sure to bring radicals.

After I gave each of my team an opportunity to speak, I addressed the issue of enslaving children. It is always hard to determine how men in this society perceive what I say. When they listen, they stare stoically. When they disagree, however, they glare. This usually happens when I explain that women and men are created equal by God. Sadly, in many of the societies in which I operate, women are treated as inferiors or possessions.

Although we had no incidents the first day, we left early the second day due to threats by radical groups made to the local police. Because those groups had the ability to lob mortars into our gatherings and have snipers target the exits, an early adjournment seemed prudent. After I delivered the final message on the value of children, we were whisked away to our accommodations where Emanuel took a call during dinner.

"Dad, we have a situation."

He told us the story of three girls, ages eleven, thirteen, and fifteen. They had been sold by their mother to a man who needed housekeepers, but as was common, they also became his sexual property. Their job was to clean and do all other domestic chores. His wife hated the girls and beat them often. The man impregnated the oldest girl when she was twelve years old, and she gave birth at thirteen. When the child was born, the man and his wife kept the baby and sold the girls to a brothel where they survived two years of constant abuse.

Emanuel's security team heard about the case and rescued the girls. The team took the girls back to their mother, not realizing it was she who sold them in the first place. Within days, she sold them again, this time to three different families.

The caller told Emanuel the girls had stopped by one of the sewing areas—a place set up by a local church where women could train to be seamstresses.

Emanuel was breathless. "Dad, can we rescue them?"

"Yes, we can, Emanuel. Have someone pick them up and bring them here. We will talk to them to find out exactly what's happening. Then we'll take them to a distant village and they will start a new life."

Half an hour later, the three girls were sitting on a couch surrounded by our team, including Emanuel's wife, Sara. One look told me they had endured hell. The oldest was beautiful, but her face was etched with sorrow. The younger two had similar expressions but looked healthier. They were covered from neck to ankles in traditional garb, and they each wore a long scarf that covered their heads and necks.

"If you like, you may remove your scarves," Emanuel's wife said gently.

They hesitated, then slowly unwound the scarves and rested them on their shoulders.

"I rescue children," said Emanuel. "That is why I brought you here. Would you like to live in a place where you can go to school and be free?"

This was a profound moment for these children. Enduring all they had suffered, asking them to trust one more time—to trust foreign men and their promise of a better life. . . . Only the resilient hope of a child could give them the courage to even consider our offer.

The three girls shifted in their chairs, looking down as if to process all of this. After a moment, the oldest exchanged glances with the other two, then shifted her gaze to Emanuel. There was an intensity in her eyes. In a monumental leap of faith, she nodded, making what could have been her last decision on earth. Then in a firm voice, she said something to Emanuel which he translated.

"Dad, they want to go far, far away."

Robert had tears in his eyes. Emanuel made a call. A driver was coming to pick the girls up. Adoring these precious girls, I could not imagine the abuse inflicted upon them. Now, they were about to leave all they knew to embark on a journey to a new life. What faith they had! *Blessed are the children.*

The girls were whisked away within the hour, and none too soon, as it turned out. The next morning, the local police stopped by asking about them. The mother knew her girls had stopped by the sewing center, and she accused Emanuel of sheltering them.

"Sir, I have no idea where the girls are," intoned Emanuel to the skeptical police.

And. . .it was true. He was clueless. The people who took the girls to a new life did not tell Emanuel where they were going, just as he had prearranged.

Locked and Hidden

The next day, we headed out to a distant brickfield where we wandered around talking to the slaves. When the owner didn't appear, we went looking and found him taking refuge from the sun under the awning of his porch. He was talking with his two adult sons. A *father-and-son slavery business*—nice.

As usual, some of the slaves gathered around us, wondering if they would be rescued.

"Please have mercy on us," cried a young mother holding her baby. "Take pity on us. Rescue us so our children will have a good life."

The owner, a large man, slow of wit but of immense bravado, immediately went into a stumbling offensive.

"Get out of here. They won't save you. Get back to work or you'll see what will happen to you!"

"We have been working here for thirty years," cried an older woman. Then turning to the owner, "All people here work for generations. You are selling your bricks at a high price, and we work hard for you, but you don't take care of us. We never have money to give back to you, and that's why we are slaves. We have been working all our lives—I've been working for you since I was a child, and even my children work for you, but we have no food to fill our bellies."

Turning away from her with studied contempt, the heavy-lidded eyes exploded with rage. "You cannot take these slaves. They will never leave here. Never!"

Jody, ever the tactician, stood quietly by one of the sons at the edge of the porch. When the son laid his phone on the ground beside a puddle, Jody casually kicked it into the water. It made a satisfying PLOP! The son gasped.

I gave Jody the "behave yourself" look and he shrugged. More and more, I was appreciating the benefits of trained operators.

As our confrontation with the owner continued, it was Eric who supplied the final element to our victory. "Guys, come over here," he hollered. "You're not going to believe this."

We followed him to a locked metal shed about twenty-foot square. A moaning, whimpering sound was coming from inside.

"There are children in here! I hear them," cried Eric.

A hammer appeared and Eric broke the lock with one vicious arc. The door was shoved open. I looked inside and screamed, "Oh my God!"

Several children, some young men, and a woman were huddled in a shed that must have been a sweltering 130°F. We were forced to turn away as the stench of human feces and ammonia wafted from the oven-like tomb.

We helped them out—many could not stand—and gave them water. We knew that owners often lock slaves in sheds as punishment.

"How long have you been here?" Emanuel asked.

"Many days."

"Without water? Food?"

"No sir. The owner locked us in here for punishment. Can you help this woman? She was beaten."

"Yes, of course." I said. "What was her crime?"

"She was helping the children whose parents died."

I was beyond reason at this point. The only question in my mind was how many slaves we could rescue.

Marching back to the owner's porch, Eric raised the broken lock like a trophy as the outraged owner cursed us for interfering in his business. Jody closed in on the owner, standing close and blowing on the owner's neck with a menacing grimace.

"You locked them in there because they helped the orphans?" I charged. "I should lock you in there. Breathe your own excrement for a week."

"These people would not work," sputtered the owner, his bravado dissolving as the words faded in the air

"You could kill them!" I said. "If you want people to work well, you have to treat them well." *Surely, there is a shred of common sense in this monster.*

"Next time we will treat them well," said the owner, looking down.

"We will come back and check," I said with a glare.

"Prove you're gonna do that," said Eric. "Bring us the locks to the shed."

"These people are slaves," said the owner. "If they don't work, we must punish them. But we will not lock them up."

"Well, we want the locks," said Eric. "Give us the locks—NOW!"

The owner nodded to his son, who returned with a handful of locks and chains.

"We have been speaking to government officials," I said. "There is going to be a change in this nation. If you don't take care of your people, we will cause problems for you. Do you understand?"

"Okay. I understand," he said slowly.

"We will be back. I promise you."

Emanuel motioned for me, then whispered that he had picked out two families that needed immediate medical care. They were top priorities for rescue. With the damning evidence before him, the owner was given no choice. We threw some money on the table, kicked in an extra dollar for the water-logged cell phone, and took the slaves to new beginnings.

Driving back with the two families and the children Eric found in the shed, our team discussed the starvation that we saw among the slaves. We decided to return the next day with a truck full of fifty-pound bags of rice to the families we were unable to rescue.

Arriving at the brick kiln the following morning, the slaves swarmed the truck. Watching them carry the bags of rice away, I wondered if the slave owners would beat them as soon as we left. We couldn't do any more for them at this point. We had no place for them, other than in our hearts.

At Our Doorstep

Back at our base of operations, we were resting when Eric came to my room. "Bruce, you need to see this," he said through tears.

I went outside with him and Emanuel and was overwhelmed at the sight of hundreds of slaves—runaways looking for freedom. Emanuel talked to some of them and their voices cried out as one.

"I was married, but my husband was killed. We walked five hours to get here. We have nothing to eat or to feed our children. We have no hope. Our desire is to send our children to school, but we cannot."

"Every day we are beaten and abused. Our lives are like animals."

"We have no food for our children. We eat the garbage."

"For eight days we have not eaten. Every day we are beaten."

"Day and night we work. We must have rest."

"Days ago, my brother got sick and could not work. But they screamed at him: 'You are a slave because we gave your family money.'"

"We are hungry—starving—and have nothing to eat. Please help."

"Our children are crying for milk, but all they can drink is the dirty water. Our children at night are crying, but how can we give them anything?"

"My father is sick; my mother is blind. Pray that my mother is healed. She needs medicine, but we cannot buy it."

"We have no house to live in. We have to sleep on the ground outside with no roof. They beat us and abuse us."

"My sister is abused every day by the owners."

"Our children cannot work, but they are forced to work. We are suffering. Help us, have mercy on us, give us freedom, rescue us."

I shook my head, trying to process it all. "What are they doing here, Emanuel?"

"Dad," said Emanuel, "They heard there were people here freeing slaves. They have come for freedom."

"What do we do?"

"Dad, we can only feed them and send them away," he said, his voice breaking with emotion. "There are too many."

"Can we give them each a bag of rice?"

"Dad, that is a lot of rice. We don't have it."

"We need to send them away with something. Buy the rice. I'll find the money."

An hour later, a large truck arrived loaded with fifty-pound bags. We passed the rice out to the people. They placed them on their heads and walked away, saddened because we could not rescue them. Later, more slaves showed up. Eric opened my door and burst into tears when he came to tell me. More rice was given, and we passed word around: "We can't take everyone who walks away from the brickfields. At least, not yet."

Indeed, exactly what we'd hoped for was beginning. Slaves were beginning to think they did not have to be slaves, that freedom was available to all. Given their lack of education and minority status, however, their society was not ready for a mass exodus of indebted slaves. For now, we were restricted to cases of acute suffering—families and children in abject conditions, the worst of the worst.

As the last crowd dispersed with their rice, Emanuel got word of children in need of immediate rescue. This usually meant sex trafficking—girls being sold off and shipped to another country. We mobilized and arrived at a school built next to a brick kiln that allowed slave children to attend in the evenings. Emanuel told me that some of these children were severely abused, and several of the pretty girls would soon be taken from their families and sold to brothels.

Our local sources directed us to a room where we found forty children waiting pensively—some local kids and some brick kiln kids. This was their few hours of reprieve from a horrible situation. We walked in, addressed the teacher, and explained our presence. She understood.

Emanuel signed deeply. "Dad, pick out a few of the girls and we will get them to safety.

"Are you serious? Which ones are in danger, Emanuel?"

"All of them, Dad," Emanuel said sadly. "But we can only take a few now. We'll come back for the rest later. The girls' families are also enslaved. We will need to get them also, but tomorrow."

How does one pick out of so many that need to be free?

Eric reached for a young girl that reminded him of his daughter and I noticed a little girl sitting close to me. With no other criteria, we lifted these precious souls into our arms. At Emanuel's prompting, they sang us their names:

"Nedah."

"Nehah."

This galvanized my heart. "Emanuel, can we come back and get more?"

"Maybe," he said nervously. "I don't know. This owner is very dangerous. We will get out as many as possible. But Dad, let's take these two for now."

I embraced the precious cargo and left in tears, my heart torn for those I could rescue and those I could not. We left the school carrying Nedah and Nehah, and found the owner next door at the brick kiln. Seeing the girls in our arms, his eyes blazed with fury.

"You cannot take the girls!" he declared before we could speak. "They owe me money!"

"How does a five-year-old child owe you money?" I demanded, stepping closer and deepening my voice. I never yelled during these confrontations; I just grew more direct. Volume—and its cousin anger—is a play of the desperate. Understood correctly by an informed opponent, it means you're out of options. Yelling is not your best card; it's your last card.

"Their families owe me money!" blustered the owner. "We have no walls here. But we bought the entire family. They belong to us."

Aaron kept the video camera rolling, the pressure mounting, the owner eyeing the lens and choosing his words with greater care.

"We are taking these girls," I declared.

In a fury, the owner tore open his debt book and stabbed a fat finger at the handwritten entries of the accumulated charges that these child miscreants had amassed over their vast lifetimes.

"Here! They . . . they owe me for food," he sputtered.

"What food? They beg in the village every night. Look at them. They're starving!"

"They owe me for water!"

"You bloody beast. They drink from a puddle!"

"They owe me for their parent's debts."

It was here that I drove my final point into his black heart.

"And where are their parents? You worked them to death, didn't you? Bastard!"

"Dad, we'll get them," pleaded a nervous Emanuel.

"Translate it, Emanuel!"

I always suspected there were times when Emanuel did not interpret my exact words, that he softened them to something less confrontational. When I spoke aggressively and Emanuel translated it to an owner, I did not always see the reaction I expected. For all I knew, my biting invective: "A pox on you and your spawn of vipers!" was being translated to: "My warmest regards to your lovely family."

Still, Emanuel kept us out of more trouble than I fully appreciated. This time, however, I was sure he translated it precisely, because the owner's eyes grew large as teacups. *Nobody's ever talked back to this guy before, have they?*

Seizing the moment of shock, Emanuel demanded: "Give me the numbers for Nedah and Nehah."

The indignant owner read off the sums. In a perfect bluff, Emanuel scoffed, threw some money on the counter—pennies on the dollar—and we walked out with the girls, listening for footsteps behind us that, to our relief, never materialized. Clearly, the owner was glad to see us leave. It wasn't even a fair fight.

Riding in Emanuel's car, Eric and I sat in the back with Nehah and Nedah. Nehah was quiet, but Nedah was a chatterbox with the cutest voice. She stood up to see what was going on. As Emanuel drove, he talked with her, asking her many questions until he burst out laughing.

"Emanuel, what's she saying?" I asked.

"I told her she is free and we will get her family, too, and make them safe. I asked her if she wanted to go to school, and she said 'Yes.' But she also asked for a mobile phone, some candy, and jewelry."

This brought some much-needed laughter from the team. Nehah and Nedah were taken to Emanuel's home where his wife made them a meal and loved on them. They ended up staying with Emanuel's family for several weeks until we were able to get both of their families out and set them up with businesses, then the girls went to live with them.

With dozens and dozens of slaves freed on this journey, we had learned the rescue process better and would return to rescue hundreds more. We knew we'd never be able to rescue every slave in every country, but we were making a change. Deep fissures were forming in the minds of key people. Change was coming. It had to. And we continued to do our part in striking blows against this evil.

Seven children rescued from hard labor eat their first healthy meal.

12

An Inconvenient Poison

SEVEN BRICK KILN OWNERS SAT IN A CIRCLE with Emanuel and me sitting across from them. They were dressed in traditional Pakistani fashion: loose-fitting pants, shirts to the knees, and scowls. One man wore glasses and looked intelligent—no mean feat for this group of criminals.

They had convened this impromptu gathering at a local brick kiln to confront me. Apparently, they knew we were coming to the area. I wasn't surprised. The local police were deep in their pockets. My team members, Robert and Bob, flanked me on either side. Robert was the pastor and stalwart friend who accompanied me on many rescues. Bob was a world traveler, a missionary, and a former business person with a heart to help unfortunate people. He was in his mid-fifties, with a short, average build and a full head of hair.

Joining us in the circle, Aaron danced around doing his camera magic while we sat on plastic chairs, our security team maintaining a wide perimeter. Given the choice between Aaron's video camera or the AK-47s carried by our guards, I think I'd go with the camera. Its effectiveness at bringing conviction to sordid souls was profound.

Someone brought tea and cookies and sat them on a small table in the middle of our circle.

"Please have some tea with us," one of the owners offered.

I noticed that none of the owners touched the tea. They didn't even look at it. "No, thank you. Not today," I replied.

It was time to get down to business. The leader, a short man with a protruding belly, spoke with a commanding air. "Why did you come here?" he demanded. Answering through Emanuel, I said tersely. "We are here to take the children away from laboring in your brick kiln."

As Emanuel interpreted, Aaron panned the camera across the bearded faces. The owners pretended to check their phones, look off to the side, or check the straps on their sandals. *Funny how sandals suddenly 'come loose.'*

"We are here to help the children who have no parents," I said, causing a stir among this reticent bunch. "And we are going to put this video on the news to show that these children are being held against their will."

"No, no! They are not our slaves," cried the suddenly amenable leader, waving his arms expansively. "I don't know why the children are here; everybody has their kids working here."

"You know very well, because the children are your slaves."

"No! They are free. Take them if you want."

"Okay then, we will take the children," I said with exaggerated gratitude. *That was too easy! Something's up.*

"What are you thinking, Emanuel?"

"Dad, we should go now!" he whispered.

Needing no further encouragement—Emanuel knew his culture and these men in particular—we rounded up twenty-nine slave children into the vans. The owners smiled expansively now, as the camera recorded everything. *Liars!* I knew they were seething, but would not show it as long as the potential of exposure loomed over them.

The children filed past us; their heads bowed like wheat stalks after a storm. Many were frail and would not have lasted much longer. With the last child safely loaded, our security team collapsed the perimeter, entered their vehicle, and our caravan sped away. We planned to meet later at a safe place. I was excited that the children would now get health care, food, clothes, a new life, and most of all: freedom.

A Dish Best Served Cold

Thinking we were done with these menacing owners, while the children were driven to a safe house, Emanuel drove the team to a local restaurant. We were all hungry; it had been a long day. Driving to the edge of the city, Emanuel parked along the main road. Our team felt exposed along a busy street, but Emanuel said we were fine. He led us into a small restaurant and immediately, the uneasiness we felt along the road intensified. It was not like the nicer places we go to, but a simpler, more basic place. The staff seemed nervous as the customers eyed us with disdain.

Large windows faced the street, making it easy for anyone walking by to see the foreigners. Strange as it may seem, not everybody in this sweltering country was cool with us rescuing their slave children and depriving the primitive economy of cheap labor. Our security guys stationed themselves both inside and out, and did not seem unusually worried. (For security guys, that is.)

"Emanuel, is this place safe?"

"It's okay, Dad," Emanuel assured me.

"Well, we're hungry. Let's eat and get out of here," I said, calming everyone but myself.

We ordered food, and it was brought to our table by the nervous staff. As we ate, they stood nearby and stared at us. When we left the restaurant, I asked Emanuel, "You sure this was a good idea?"

"Yes, Dad. They just never see Americans here."

"Well, they might never see them again."

And perhaps that was the intent.

Not long after returning to Emanuel's home, he became ill. Thinking it was because of bad food, he went to bed to sleep it off. An hour later, he was pounding at my door.

"Dad. I'm very sick. I'm going to the hospital. Youssef will take me."

Youssef is Emanuel's brother, the brains behind the scenes. While Emanuel is the lead guy for us, it is Youssef who arranges security, logistics, and payroll.

I went back to sleep and started feeling a burning sensation in my abdomen. It was like coming down with a fever. Robert rushed into my room and told me Aaron was throwing up violently. I grew sicker as the night wore on. At one point, woozy and confused, I heard gunfire and sent a text to a friend in the United States that read as if we were under attack. I did not clarify that the gunfire was distant and not a threat to us. One of my former team members, Eric, received a copy of the text. Thinking our lives were in peril, he sprang to action, arranging for a volunteer team to come to our aid.

In the morning, still disoriented, I read the text string and realized what I'd instigated. Through blurry vision, I clarified in texts to Eric that I did not think there was an immediate threat. Eric was upset. He had set a rescue operation in motion, and his reputation was on the line. Fortunately, he worked things out with the special ops group and they remained at the ready if needed.

Still confused and my intestines burning, I took some probiotics and some Pepto—anything to help—and waited for nature to take its course. I felt like a fallen gladiator waiting for a thumbs up or down from the emperor.

There was little we could do that morning without Emanuel. Youssef gave us sporadic updates on his condition, and it was not good. He was in intensive care with a fever of 105°F. The doctor eventually concluded that it was poison. He was discharged three days later, still very weak. We later found out that both Emanuel and I had contracts on our lives and that our pictures had been passed around the areas we frequented. No wonder the restaurant staff was jittery. Of all the seedy joints in all the towns in all of Pakistan, Public Enemies One and Two just walked into theirs. And there was a bounty on our heads.

Back to the Fray

I was improving, and Aaron had recovered. I still felt strange, though. When Emanuel returned home, he rested a few days and decided he wanted to do one more rescue before my team and I returned home. He was tough.

Being raised on the streets, he had to be. I was surprised he wanted to go; he still seemed weak. Still, he could not do these rescues effectively without us. The one time he tried to go it alone, the owners threw bricks at him, smashing his car windows and crushing the doors. The car was totaled. He needed us as much as we needed him.

I took an assessment of our situation. Emanuel weak, me barely walking, Bob, Robert, and Aaron okay but inexperienced. Clearly, we were in perfect shape for a human rescue. We grabbed Youssef and the security detail and headed out.

Based on some pre-op intel from one of Emanuel's friends, we drove ninety minutes to an area Emanuel had never been to before. The brickfield was different than others we knew of—it was nicer, if you could call a place that tortured children *nice*. The porch was tiled and modern. A thin man dressed all in white and wearing a turban greeted us regally as we exited the vehicles. He wore wire-rim glasses and had an air of majesty about him. I judged him to be in his thirties. He spoke first, as if we had nothing of value to say to him. He told us he was calling his father to come to talk to us. He and his father were partners in the brick business.

After several awkward moments, during which Emanuel told him we were taking some slaves to get food and medical care, the father arrived in an expensive SUV. The front license plate revealed that he was the head of a regional justice organization.

Interesting. . . . Justice for whom?

The man's father was also wearing white, a turban, and had a trimmed white beard. He was stocky, looked to be in his fifties, and carried himself with authority. We met him at the porch, where he greeted us with a slight smile. He knew he was king, and no one would dare disturb his kingdom. He and his son sat at a small table while our team sat in a semi-circle on the other side. The father said something to one of his servants and cookies and tea appeared.

"Where are you from?" he demanded before I could speak.

"We are from South Africa," I lied.

Bob and Robert stayed silent while Aaron worked the camera.

"Have you been to South Africa?" I asked.

"No, but if I would go, I would start brick kilns there," he said with an arrogant laugh.

Emanuel said something in Urdu that clearly agitated him. Seizing the moment—actions speak louder than words— I got up, grabbed the plate of cookies and offered them first to the father and then the son. They declined, as I expected. Perhaps I had defiled them.

Oh well, no cookies for you.

After I sat down, the father, perhaps not wishing to waste any more time on us, grew belligerent.

"I am a very powerful man in this nation. I have friends at high levels of leadership in the government."

I was not impressed.

"Listen," I said. "You like to make money; who doesn't? But slavery will end soon, and you should consider using machinery to make the bricks using paid employees instead of slave labor."

"Never! We own these people and they work for us. They are our machines. That is how things are done here. We can own Christians and any other infidel. It is our way."

I leaned over to Emanuel. "Well, this is going nowhere fast."

"It always does, Dad."

We knew there was no reasoning with these slave owners. For them to give up slaves—to see things differently—meant loss of profit and prestige. To change your view of enslaving humans meant deviating from the cultural mores that say Christians are created for slavery. Violating that creed could mean death or worse—excommunication. Buoyed by social acceptance, these people thrive by using minorities as tools and work animals, and they see nothing wrong with it. In the conversations I've had with slave owners, they have all indicated it is okay to own humans, and they believe their religion justifies it.

I stared at this belligerent father-son team and grew determined.

"We are taking families with us, those who need medical care," I commanded. "And these children need to go to school."

"No, never! They owe us money," declared the son.

Aaron moved in closer with the video camera. Both father and son glanced at the camera and looked away. *Suddenly shy, are we?* More powerful than our security team's firearms was the threat of exposure. A proverb flashed in my mind: "Everyone who does evil hates the light, and will not come into the light for fear that their deeds will be exposed."

Suddenly impatient, Emanuel walked over to two slave families, handed the father of each a small amount of money, and told them to give it to the owner. The slaves couldn't know this, but it was a small fraction of what the convoluted books of generational slavery said they owed— the accumulated debt of lifetimes.

With heads bowed—they still could not make eye contact with their enslavers—each slave handed the paltry sum to the owner. The father snapped it from the men's hands and shoved it at his son. His rage was palatable. *I love the smell of pissed off owners. It smells like victory.*

Still, intimidation has a short shelf life, and Emanuel knew it better than any of us. We hustled the two families into the van and got out of there. We knew phone calls were being placed even as we drove off. *Crap, this could get real, fast.* As soon as we returned home the death calls to Emanuel's phone started rolling in. How they got his number so quickly was anybody's guess. The calls were detailed—they knew of Emanuel, his family, their home, his vulnerability. He made a call to his police friend, and soon the area was on high alert.

It was time for us to go back to the United States. Emanuel was still weak, so we decided to drive to the airport a little early. No better time to make a quick exit than now!

On the flight home, the intestinal burning returned with a vengeance. Considering what Emanuel had gone through, I was worried. Back home, my doctor said I had a bacterial infection. Whatever poison we ingested, it had really messed up my system.

Emanuel called a few days later and said the death threats continued, but he was standing strong and was not afraid.

"Dad, they want you dead; they want me dead. I am not afraid. If I die, I will die for the Lord."

"Yes, Emanuel. And if we live, we live for the Lord!"

"Yes, Dad. Glory to God!"

13

The Long Road to Freedom

No ONE CAN UNDERSTAND SLAVERY unless they have lived it. I have observed it, rescued people from it, and interviewed slaves and former slaves. I have seen thousands of people enslaved, have witnessed brutality and have seen hundreds of victims of torture. I have seen children hit with metal and bamboo rods and have heard other horrific stories I cannot erase from my mind. But I have not been a slave. I can only imagine slavery from the eyes of a liberator. And I respond accordingly, in the best ways I know, striving to be more effective.

Sitting in the kitchen of the house that was our head-quarters during this trip, we were asked to come down-stairs. A story of horror and heartache awaited us. It was an early hour of the day, around 6 a.m. The sun was barely up and we were tired from an intense day of rescues. As I descended the curving cement staircase, I saw Emanuel talking to several of his security guys.

"Emanuel, what is happening?"

"Dad, a man and his wife escaped from their enslaver. They walked seventy miles to a place they heard had freedom."

"Where are they?" I asked.

"Sitting on the couch."

I entered the room, and there was a family of four seated on a simple couch. It was a bare space with cement walls, and already very warm as the temperature outside was rising. Two children sat between their parents, all were dirty, wearing torn clothing, and their heads were tilted down.

"Dad, this woman fainted when they got to the house. She is exhausted and sick."

I knelt before them, but as is typical with slaves, they would not make eye contact. The Shalwar Kameez, or traditional clothing of the Indian sub-continent that the man wore, was once white but now was stained brown. The woman wore a similar outfit in slightly better shape, but it was also worn, torn, and faded. I gently touched the man's hand and told him that we would help, with Emanuel translating my gesture. Finally, they told us their story.

I told them they should rest, and that a hot meal was coming to them. The man still could not look up; the woman gave me a weak smile.

"Dad, if they go back, they will be killed."

"We will keep them here," I replied, somewhat overwhelmed at how many runaway slaves were beginning to show up. Every day, more and more slaves were hearing that there was hope, that there were people who had come to help. While we were out freeing slaves in the brickfields, runaways were showing up at the house. The best we could do for many was to give them a large bag of rice and tell them we would try to come for them later. There were just so many.

With the family fed, we recorded their story. Our translator was a man I had not worked with before, but he seemed genuine. Early in the interview, my interpreter stopped abruptly and burst into tears. I waited. I knew it would be hard but we needed to know what they told him. Standing before this broken couple, I readied myself to continue the interview.

"I think I can go on now," he said.

"What did they tell you?"

He began to weep again and barely got the words out.

"This couple . . . has been severely tortured by the owner. The owner uses . . . he uses their son for sex. He sodomizes him daily. The parents were raped repeatedly when they were younger. Now they watch their children being raped. They get beaten with rods every day."

With the camera still recording, I asked the family if they wanted their story to be heard. We explained that they did not have to say anything, we would still make them free.

Slaves like this have no understanding of the world, only their limited existence as slaves. The man said quietly that he wanted people to know what was happening to slaves like them. The look in his eyes seared my heart. Such pain. No hope. I cried.

Every time I help free a slave, a new resolve emerges. Gazing at this couple, I was filled with compassion, then a righteous anger rose within me. Again, Emanuel explained that the owner of the brickfield these slaves had escaped from was a well-known, especially vile man.

Taking Emanuel aside, I said, "We need to get these slaves to a new home, as soon as possible."

"The owner is a very powerful man, Dad. I'm not sure what to do," Emanuel replied tensely.

"Does he know where they went?"

"No, I don't think so. And Dad, he can never find out we helped them."

"Well, if he doesn't know, then let's make them disappear to a new life."

"Okay, Dad. We'll do this. We'll find a way," said Emanuel, wringing his hands.

We returned to the living room where the family remained huddled together and spoke words of life to them.

"We are taking you to a new life, to a place where you will no longer be slaves."

The father shuddered, buried his face in his hands and wept. The mother, tears filling her eyes, looked up and nodded. I imagine the realization had set in that their children would no longer be abused.

Once again, food was brought to them, and we left so they could enjoy another hot meal. I looked through a gap in the curtain. They were talking to each other as they ate. They had not eaten in days.

The team was happy that we could make this couple free and get them into a new life. With all of the tragedy we experience and the horrible situations we encounter, knowing we are setting so many people free from the confinement of slavery is an emotion hard to describe. One minute a person has no rights, no hope, no future, and the next they are free.

As we watched the family load into a vehicle to be taken to a new life, the woman turned to me and said something.

What, I do not know, but the look in her eyes told me she was happy. Our eyes followed the van as it went down the alleyway and disappeared around the corner.

Our hearts were full.

PART II
A Professional Approach

14

Full Disclosure

WE HAVE RESCUED THOUSANDS OF VICTIMS but we did not put enough bad guys away. What we did do is hurt them economically, close down businesses, expose them, help change a few laws, and according to a high-level government official in one country, we influenced the movement of ordinary people into rescuing victims of slavery.

We have educated police, military, and thousands of others on the facts and dynamics of human trafficking.

We have trained dozens to be rescue operators and several other organizations were formed from former team members and students.

There were times I felt rage towards the perpetrators, but I always felt such deep love for the captives. There were times I hit the floor in intense prayer so I could find a way through the pain and anger, and also to ask God to increase my heart of love so I could navigate the hostile world of slavery and trafficking. I needed to reconcile my warrior side and my compassionate side as we witnessed the worst of mankind.

Personally, I think human traffickers deserve the death penalty. Presently, however, I seem to be of the minority opinion, and possibly rightly so. The elimination of every sponsor of slavery would only open the way for others. We have to get to the roots of the issue. Slavery, in any form, is vile to both victim and perpetrator. It dehumanizes the victim to such an extent that all hope is lost and their dignity is no more. It also dehumanizes the abuser until they no longer have a conscience. In their morally-debased condition, they become easy prey to the very evil that is using them to afflict others. In truth, the true victim is humankind, and the cause is evil itself.

15

A New Attitude

CONTINUALLY ASSESSING ONE'S CAPABILITIES AND DEFICIENCIES is key to meeting any challenge. When those challenges pertain to life and death—yours and the people you are trying to help—advanced preparation is imperative. I knew I was fit and trim, a professional adventurer who could meet the wilderness on its own terms. But for future rescues, I needed to raise my performance level. We were having a measure of success, but this was leading us deeper and deeper into the entrenched slavery culture, and we were meeting greater resistance. I realized that I needed better-trained team members. I need stalwart warriors who understood what we were up against, people who could operate in the culture and achieve the objective without causing more problems than we came to solve. It was time to up my game.

So, in 2011, I enrolled in a two-week executive protection course. I knew it could not train me in all that I needed, but it would highlight my weaknesses and indicate where I needed to focus my training in the coming months prior to our next rescue. It would also teach me what to look for in future team members.

In the course, we were taught a variety of protective, defensive, and technical skills. We learned physical conditioning in ways I hadn't previously appreciated. We were taught firearms, situational awareness, hand-to-hand combat, defensive driving and maneuvering, and skills such as reading body language, interrogation techniques, surveillance and technology, how to move with your client, creating safe environments, and many other skills.

No longer merely humanitarians, from this moment forward our trips took on a more professional approach.

I recently heard a quote by Dr. Jordan Peterson that sums up our situation beautifully. Being somewhat of an aggressive individual—he is an academic psychologist and outspoken critic of the far-left—he was never comfortable with Jesus's words: "Blessed are the meek, for they shall inherit the earth." What Peterson wanted to know was this: What is to be admired about being meek? Then he heard an interpretation of the word *meek* from the original language, and it all made sense. *Meek*, in the sense that Jesus used it, means "he who has a sword and knows how to use it, but keeps it sheathed until absolutely necessary."[8]

We were going into some of the most dangerous areas in the world, intent on rescuing its most valuable possession—human labor. Well-trained and equipped, we were not going to pick a fight, but we could defend ourselves and the slaves we rescued if necessary. We were going as the meek.

---

[8] "Jordan Peterson: The Meek Shall Inherit the Earth (a Misunderstood Phrase)," YouTube (Old Truths, September 20, 2018), https://www.youtube.com/watch?v=cct98wRv3SY&t=11s.

Remarkably, amidst all our preparation, our most potent weapon was the video camera. There is something about the craven evil of a corrupt soul that cowers in the presence of righteousness. Good will always overcome evil. But to do so, good must confront evil.

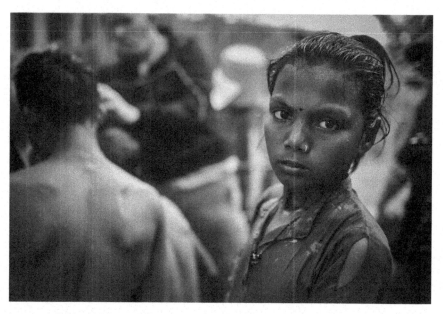

Just cleaned up from being covered head to toe with mud, a newly freed girl wonders what is to come.

16

Rules of Engagement

As our skills and requirements evolved, I realized the necessity of defining our Rules of Engagement (ROE) for all team members.

*****

"Rules of Engagement are the internal rules or directives that define the circumstances, conditions, degree, and manner in which the use of force, or actions that might be construed as provocative, may be applied.[1][9] They provide authorization for and/or limits on, among other things, the use of force and the employment of certain specific capabilities."[10]

At Children's Rescue Initiative, we are often found in dangerous and confrontative situations in our mission to release children and adults from the captivity of slavery.

First and foremost is the capacity of the team leader and team members to mitigate the possibility of violence and aggression.

---

[9] "MC 362/1, NATO Rules of Engagement," Govtribe.com, August 1, 2016, https://govtribe.com/file/government-file/rfpactsact1646-mc-362-1-nato-roe-dot-pdf.

[10] "Rules of Engagement," Wikipedia (Wikimedia Foundation, March 18, 2022), https://en.wikipedia.org/wiki/Rules_of_engagement.

The main priority is to release captives and to minimize the possibility of a physical confrontation. While the possibility of aggression on the part of a slave owner, madam, employee of, clients, or bystanders is real and possible, it is the duty of the team leader and team members to consider the consequences of ALL actions while on a rescue operation, from wheels up, to wheels down, to the actual rescue itself. These consequences could directly affect our local indigenous team and also the future of CRI.

1) At no time is any team member to harm anyone due to temper, emotions, or a justification that they deserve it.

2) At no time is any team member to instigate the team to do violence.

3) Engagement of a potential threat: If any person touches a team member in a non-friendly way, threatens by approach, yields a weapon with perceived intent of harm, strikes, pushes, surrounds, or is close enough that the intent is clear, engagement is permitted with these stipulations:

   a) Using only enough force to stop the problem, and
   b) Using enough counterforce to be able to make an exit.

17

Face to Face with Terrorism

AFTER MONTHS AT HOME raising funds and organizing, Tom, Chris, and I arrived in Pakistan, full of hope and zeal, ready to make an impact. I was looking forward to operating with a team of professionals. I knew we could not do what we did—storm these bastions of enslavement and rob them of their human capital—if the slave owners were not corrupt. In the contest of wills, righteousness beats evil every time. The trouble was, corruption in this country had a way of multiplying.

Tom had heard one of my talks and sought me out. A former soldier and specialist in small arms, he operated with an intensity that stemmed from his deep passion to see children removed from suffering. Tom was my best-trained team member—fit, trim, powerful, and dark-complected, he was at home in any conflict in any corner of the world. We would need him in our corner.

Tom and I met when he heard about the work we did. Living in the same area, we started to train together. Tom had a background in Russian Systema, the combat fighting system of the Russian Spetsnaz (Special Operations Forces), so I started learning from him. My background was in Krav Maga and a few other styles. It was all great training for our work.

Chris was new to us, and although I checked him out thoroughly, he lacked some training. Still, he made up for it with youth and enthusiasm. Nothing that experience couldn't cure. I was glad to have him along with us. He was a quiet soul, a patient observer. Blonde, svelte, and intuitive, I could count on his support in hostile situations when slave owners took a dim view to our confiscation of their illegal property. Chris's main job was to operate the camera—the most potent weapon in our arsenal. When Jesus said: "All who do evil hate the light and refuse to go near it for fear their sins will be exposed", I am sure he meant the light of a video camera. That is why Chris's camera, with its logo of a world-renown news organization, was such a threat to the despicable bastards of the brick kilns. We were going in country to do business, and Chris was all business.

Pakistan is a conflicted country, with slavery as one of its not-so-hidden secrets. We were eager to get to work exposing it, but upon arrival, Emanuel told us to rest. We would start early the next morning. After forty hours of travel and an eleven-hour time difference, it took a few days to be fully adjusted, so resting was good advice, even to a trio of hopped-up avengers. The adrenaline was strong even if the flesh was exhausted.

After a good night's rest, the team and I convened over breakfast to discuss the day's game plan. One of our local assets had identified a brick kiln that had a number of orphan slave children. After listening to his appeal, we decided on a gameplan that took advantage of our disorientation with the time zone. We would rise hours before dawn, load the vans—with our team, security, and space for the rescued orphans—and breach the brick kiln's perimeter at dawn.

We had learned by now that local operators were key to supplying good intel. Being known in their community meant they were in constant danger, however. Several of our contacts were discovered and beaten for their service, a few severely. Most endured and continued working for us; a few left town for their own safety and that of their families.

We navigated through the city's endless traffic and smog. Tom was fired up. He stared out the window at the passing panorama of rickshaws, motorbikes, and expensive SUVs. He was talking freely, unconcerned whether anyone was listening or not.

We finally entered the countryside where we turned onto a rough dirt lane. The driver maneuvered the car carefully through ruts, steered clear of wandering water buffalo, and drove the 400-yard dirt road to the brick kiln.

Part of our pre-trip planning involved the sharing of weaponry. Tom and I would swap a Beretta 9mm and an AK-47 depending on who was in the front seat. It was a little easier to maneuver the AK in the front seat, even though the rifle was too long to raise easily. It was not ideal, but it was what we had—the true meaning the phrase *riding shotgun.*

Driving the dirt road kicked up a cloud of dust. As we approached the kiln, we saw the unwilling laborers toiling in the heat of daybreak. A few children peeked over the stacked bricks to see who was coming, alerted by the sound of tires on gravel. We parked our vehicles by a stack of bricks in the shadows of the brick kiln, its smokestack discharging dark, billowing smoke that filled the sky. The whole scene felt surreal, like something out of Dante's *Inferno*— "Abandon hope, all ye who enter here." *Well . . . not today.*

We strode through the brickfield unimpeded, two of Emanuel's guys carrying video cameras, Emanuel speaking with the slaves in Urdu, and our armed-to-the-teeth security looking like they came from a small town called "Kick Ass" and were feeling mighty homesick. Emanuel chose three families who seemed to be in the worst shape. One mother was crippled from polio in her foot and limbed furiously to keep from being left behind. Another woman said she was one hundred years old. She told us she had prayed her whole life to be free; she wanted to die a free woman.

Each family had five members—at least, it appeared they were related by the initial report that Emanuel gave us. Looking at the hundred-year-old lady and those with her, it was obvious they had all suffered. Gnarled hands, deformed feet from years of work, scars and weathered faces—a living horror story etched into their weathered bodies. The other two families were the same. Dirty rags hung from their bodies as they shuffled alongside us.

We took the slaves to the owner's building to wait for his arrival. We met the assistant, a thin, nervous man with hard, darting eyes, and discovered that the door was locked. The assistant could not work the key—his hands were shaking too badly—so we broke the lock. I guess he'd never seen such a show of force on a brickfield before.

146

Bowing frantically, he ushered us in and offered refreshments, which we refused.

The owner arrived in an opulent SUV, black with tinted windows, a uniformed driver, most likely a slave, at the wheel. I knew this type of owner as soon as he stepped out: a sleazy, self-righteous man, pompous and demeaning. Our pre-op intel on the slave owner said he'd been in another country for many years running a factory with hundreds of employees. He spoke English very well. Possessing a calculating mind, he took stock of the situation—Americans, cameras, security, and expectant slaves—and responded with a force of his own: defiance. The battle was on.

"We are taking these families," I said forcefully.

He threw his head up, looked away and stated emphatically, "No! They cannot go!"

"These people are sick; they need help. It is wrong to enslave people."

"This is not my way to have slaves, but the way of God. These are my people. I treat them well."

"They are Christians, and we are taking them to freedom. You treat them like dogs."

"If you take them, you take my money," he responded, infuriated. "I will go from having seventy-two slaves to only having fifty."

Well too stinking bad!

As we continued to press him, it became clear he was holding out for what the slaves owed him. This was the place to which we had been maneuvering him. Time to make an offer he couldn't refuse.

"You have set up a system where they can never pay back what they borrow because you do not pay them for any work. So they have to borrow from you just to stay alive. Then you set such high interest that it is impossible to pay it all back. The more they work for you, the more they owe. This is diabolical."

A slight smile washed over him, heralding a sea change in tactics. "Of course, of course," he said, holding out his arms as if speaking to a savvy businessman. "What would you have me do? Do you wish to buy them back? They owe a lot of money."

It was time for the final negotiation. *You aren't going to like how this ends.*

Barking to his anxious assistant, he ordered the man to bring the debt book. The sleaze-ball made a great show of examining the records and declaring the exorbitant sums these precious people owed. I could have bought his SUV for less. This man, with his higher education and political connections, knew the game better than most. If we were to free these people, we would need to give him some amount of money to pay off their debts. We had been told by a high-ranking government official that we should always pay some money; otherwise, the owners could accuse us of stealing their property.

"I'm giving you five US dollars per person," I said firmly. "That's it. And we are leaving with the families."

While the owner bluffed and sputtered, I knelt down to a little girl in one of the families with us, handed her the cash—the price of these five families—and told her to hand it to her tormentor. One of our security guards was within arm's reach, so she was safe from any sudden violence.

I relished the moment. To have a slave girl hand him the funds was a great insult. He swiped it from her hand, hate burning in his eyes. With cameras rolling and our security guys moving, we walked the twenty-two newly freed human beings to their chariots. Five dollars a person for freedom wasn't bad considering he claimed they collectively owed him several thousand dollars. He was left with a massive deficit, one that I hoped matched his deplorable soul. The only thing that could have made me happier was if he would have had a heart attack on the spot and collapsed face down in his own blood.

There was a bit of jostling as we put all twenty-two adults and children into the van, but the highlight was when I looked into the second seat where the one-hundred-year-old woman was smiling ear to ear. That was worth everything!

Our team remained on high alert as we rode back to our base of operations, watching carefully for anyone tailing us. We scanned rooftops and general surroundings for potential ambushes. We paid special attention when we got within a mile of where we stayed. The streets were narrow, perfect for snipers, IEDs, and roadblocks. By now the community knew we were here, though how they felt about us depended on their perspective.

The freed people were taken back to a school where they got new clothes, showers, their first toilet experience, and a hot meal. Later, we met with them and talked about their new lives. Finally, we took a group picture. I stood by the one-hundred-year-old woman, and she kept touching me and smiling. I am pretty sure she was flirting; she pushed me one time and giggled. One hundred years of slavery; she was now free to live and giggle.

Priceless!

It looks like chocolate milk, but this boy is drinking water from the pond. He died soon after this picture was taken.

18

Slum Lords

CHRISTIAN SLUMS IN PAKISTAN ARE INFAMOUS for the deplorable conditions the inhabitants live in. Having only been told of the degradation in these regions, I asked Emanuel to take me to a Christian slum. What broke my heart was not the filthy environment, but the deprivation of people's lives. As we walked through the trash-strewn alleys with open sewage and makeshift tents, my senses were overwhelmed. The stench alone was staggering. *These people live in absolute squalor!* Garbage and flies were everywhere: a pathogen-rich environment seething with decay. One of the men walking with us explained that a recent rainstorm had flooded this area and a dozen children had died.

A crippled man in rags limped toward us with his children following and offered us his newborn baby and daughters. He was preparing to sell his daughters, a last act of desperation since he could barely feed them anymore. He hoped we could take them someplace better than the dark future awaiting them as human property.

Emanuel, knowing my heart, spoke before I could reply.

"No, Dad. We cannot take these children. We have no room. Also . . . look around you, Dad. We are being watched." He seemed very nervous.

As we spoke, an emaciated mother approached us, and in gracious supplications, also offered us her children, laying one at our feet.

I wanted to intervene immediately, bring these people out of the slum and get them into homes, medical care, food, and job training. But the pragmatic side of me—a side I was learning to heed—said, "Wait, *build a coalition, plan carefully, and execute the plan.*" As we left the area, I looked back at the crowd who had gathered and was overwhelmed by their flat, hollow eyes and their smiles.

A Plan of Action

That evening, determined to put actions to feelings, we met in our room and hammered out a plan for the next day's rescues. I was adamant that we would rescue the children who were about to be sold to brothels and brickfields. We couldn't save every child in every slum in Pakistan, but we could save the ones who landed at our feet—literally . . . at our feet. We also needed more rescues of slaves in the brickfields and rope factories. Finally, we discussed raiding a brothel. There were hundreds of home-based brothels in the city where we were staying alone. Children were commonly abused by twenty men a day.

The plan for the next day was to go to a brick kiln and rescue two families and several orphans, which we had heard about from our local contacts. Since we no longer had room for orphans until we got new buildings, we would have the orphans stay in the homes we provide for the families we rescue, and those families would become temporary foster parents.

Once we were in the vans and safely away from the brick kiln, we planned to visit a Christian slum to rescue the most desperate families and the children who were in danger of being sold. While they were not slaves at present, we knew the children would end up in a brothel or a brick kiln, and would most likely never leave alive. The slaves and slum dwellers would be brought back to our central home and school where we would interview them and settle them into long-term care.

We spent the next morning having breakfast at Emanuel's house, talking with three women who were previously rescued. Emanuel had nowhere to put them, so he hired them to help run the household. One mother spoke of her eight-year-old daughter, Nirmal, who had been raped by a seventy-year-old man. Suddenly, my appetite was gone.

Our caravan left for the brick kiln, a new one we had never been to before. We were in three vehicles: my team in one, an empty van for the rescued slaves, and another for our security detail. We drove for miles and entered an area far from the road.

We all noticed it, but Tom was the first to speak. "Bruce, this is dangerous. One long dirt road in and out—it'll be easy to get trapped back here."

"I agree," I said. "Let's post a security guy at the entrance to the main road."

The guy I had in mind was armed with a pump-action shotgun. Not effective for pinpoint accuracy but an excellent crowd deterrent—loud and inaccurate. *Perfect!* We'd know when trouble was coming, and trouble would know we were coming.

As we navigated the labyrinth of bricks stacked impossibly high, we found the group of what our local contact described as "orphans and children." Some were living with a grandparent due to the parent's deaths. Several other children had been beaten to death on the owner's whim.

We spread out and started taking pictures. A man identified as the administrator of the brick kiln showed up and engaged the local man who led us here. This was dangerous for our local contact—we would soon leave the area, but he lived here. He was a brave man to help us.

I approached the administrator and pointed to my team members with video cameras. "We were making a documentary on your operation, how it traps people into generational slavery, and how you abuse the slaves and kill them. Care to comment?"

He looked shocked.

"It will air on all major western news broadcasts, including BBC."

He blanched when I said "BBC." Now I was certain he would tell the owner. In fact, I was counting on it. But really, "Bruce's Broadcasting Company" was just getting started.

While the administrator hurried off to make a phone call, Chris identified two families in great need of rescue. He spoke with them while we searched for the orphans. We found them turning over bricks, their ragged clothes covered in red dust. I never get used to the sight of children who have been abused physically and sexually. It's a rush of heartbreak, rage, and compassion—a powerful elixir that drives everything I do.

When Emanuel told the families we were setting them free, one woman stood up and threw a metal brick mold on the ground with a loud clang. That was a beautiful sound. She stood defiant, her face radiant as if to say: "Finally, someone is here to get us out of this hellhole!"

I walked over, caught the edge of the brick form with my toe, and flipped it through the air, into the muddy pond used for bricks and drinking water for the slaves. It landed with a satisfying splat. Inspired, I packed another brick mold into my backpack to use for my talks back home. Looking around, I wondered if the administrator saw me do this—not that I cared. But he was lost in a growing crowd of slaves. All work had stopped in the brick kiln. Slaves were gathering from all over the field. They walked toward us, adults and children alike, to see what was happening. There were no expressions on any faces, only eager feet and wonder-filled eyes.

The owner of this kiln was obviously very wealthy, as his slave empire stretched as far as we could see. Looking out on the human misery, I wanted to hurt the bastard any way I could. Emanuel, my better half, reminded me that the owner was a very powerful man who could afford to fund a personal vendetta. I realized I could not risk any retaliation on my team or Emanuel and his family.

As our team walked the two families toward the van, a group of six girls linked hand-in-hand approached the van and spoke to Emanuel in halting tones. They looked to be in their mid-teens, still beautiful despite their horrible living conditions. I noticed the gold rings in their noses and knew exactly what their pleading voices were saying. My disgust boiled over.

"Dad, these girls are sex slaves to the owner and his brothers," said Emanuel.

"We can't leave them here, Emanuel," I said firmly.

"Come," said Emanuel to the girls. "We are going to take you out of here."

"No, we cannot leave," they cried. "He will come for us. He will torture and kill us. He has done so to many girls. Please just bring us food."

"We will take you to a place where he can't hurt you anymore," said Emanuel. "We will protect you. He will never touch you again. You will be far away. And if he tries to follow you, these men will deal with him." Emanuel pointed to our armed and ready for action security detail.

It was a compelling argument, and in the end, what choice did they really have? They looked among themselves, nodded at Emanuel, and trembling, slipped into the vehicle with the rest of the slaves.

The slaves continued to arrive. I lost count of how many there were. Some of our team kept loading the van, while Tom, Chris, Emanuel, Aaron, and I headed to a small brick building to meet the owner.

"Keep your weapons ready," said Emanuel. "He is a very powerful man; he is known for being radical and violent."

I had never seen Emanuel so nervous. We prepared ourselves to take on any situation that would arise.

"Please keep your doors unlocked and ready to go," Emanuel added.

"Yes, we are always ready," I replied.

As we approached the porch area, I saw two older men in white robes with long black beards and weathered faces. They looked professional. Introductions were made. I approached the owners and shook hands, making sure I put the squeeze into the shake. Tom, Chris, Emanuel, and I sat facing the owners. Aaron wielded the video camera, exploiting fissures of discomfort in the visages of these men who were accustomed to the cloak of anonymity.

The lead owner spoke first.

"This is my younger brother," he said, speaking excellent English.

"Where are you from?" the older brother asked.

I didn't like either one of these guys. They had evil little grins that faded as our discussion ensued. They knew we were the first foreigners in this country to take away slaves. We had been told by government officials that no one else does what we were doing. We also knew that no one ever challenged men like these. They were kings of their territories, rulers of the pond. *Well, isn't that great? We're about to upset your lily pads.*

"I am American, and these gentlemen are from all over the world," I said, pointing to my teammates.

"Would you like some lunch?" asked the lead brother.

"No, thank you for asking."

"Coca-Cola or drinks?" he asked, pointing to a large bottle of Coke.

"No, we are fine."

I really want to shove that bottle down your throat.

"We are here to help the children," I said. "We want to take these families and orphans to a new life. We are evaluating the health and justice of children. We have been all over your country helping slaves attain their freedom."

"This is good," he said, much to my surprise. Normally, we encountered aggression. Evidently, telling the administrator we were making a documentary had its desired effect. The owner knew he was on camera. *Smile for the camera!*

"We are here to help these people too," he said. "We give them jobs to care for their families."

"Yes, of course you do," I said. "We also want them to—"

"Good! Then we have no problem between us," he interrupted.

"Yes, but these people desperately need medical attention. We are going to take these two families, these girls, and the other orphans."

At the mention of the girls, the owner suddenly switched subjects.

"I was recently to South Africa on safari," he said eagerly.

This was a connecting point for me. I am always looking for ways to mitigate the danger, to diffuse the tension that occurs when we remove their means of production, and in this case, their perverted appetites.

"Yes, Africa is an interesting place. I, too, have been on safari."

"Yes, it is good," he said, studying me afresh.

Yes, I get your drift, buddy.

Chris leaned over and whispered, "Bruce, they're stalling."

He was right—it was possible they were waiting for reinforcements to arrive. That single dirt road was growing longer by the second, but the team was still loading slaves. *Just a little more time.*

"So, we will be taking several families," I said.

The owners smiled as if it did not matter. Their kingdom was close to the Christian slums. They would simply get more children. They were used to replacing slaves because of the high mortality rate. But today would be a massive financial hit. We were taking seasoned child and adult workers. We would leave them with a deficit and the knowledge that we could return at any time.

Continuing this strange exchange, the younger brother spoke up.

"Perhaps we could meet for lunch sometime."

Oh sure. Businessman to businessman. Uh huh.

"That would be a possibility," I said in my best polite voice. *Who knows? Maybe I'll learn more about how slavery works.*

Emanuel shot me a look that said: *That'll never happen, Bruce!*

Figuring that the van was filled with slaves, we said our goodbyes and sauntered casually to our vehicles so as not to create alarm. Although we walked confidently, we were way behind schedule. These owners had successfully played it out. A typical rescue should take eight minutes. This rescue, from arriving to identifying slaves, to speaking with the owners, to getting back to the van, was fifteen minutes. And the owners did not even try to negotiate or get the slaves to pay off their debts. Way too long.

Thinking this rescue could convey no more emotional trauma, we arrived at the van to find it surrounded by weeping women who were shoving their children through the open windows, begging us to take them, knowing they would never see them again. As tragic as this was, it was the only hope these children had of a decent life.

Arriving at our safehouse, we learned that forty-five freed slaves had been crammed into that fifteen-passenger van!

We returned to Emanuel's home and the adjacent school to meet with the people we rescued and see them off to their new homes. Emanuel had a system set up—upon arriving at headquarters, volunteers meet with the former slaves, feed them, issue new clothes, and figure out where they would be settled.

One of the volunteers was Amon, the little boy we rescued from the factory two years prior. I called his name, and he ran toward me, leaping into my arms and burying his head in my neck. I wanted to hold him and never let him go. I walked with him into the school courtyard where the newly freed children gathered and introduced them to Amon. He went around shaking their hands. Then I asked Faisal to pick up Amon. It was beautiful to see the first slave we saved hold Amon in the middle of the newly rescued group.

After speaking with the new rescues and figuring out the care of the children whose parents sent them alone, we were emotionally exhausted. I kept fighting back tears as I looked at the children that were pushed into the van. They would never see their parents again; their parents were still enslaved, and they would most likely die as slaves. But now, at least the children had a chance of a free life.

We helped get all forty-five precious people into vehicles to take them to their new homes. As they drove away, our team was silent, each drawn into their own emotional well of reflection. We had rescued so many, yet we had left too many more behind.

Back to the Slums

The next day, buoyed by our success at the brick kiln, I thought this would be a good time to go back to the Christian slums and rescue children before they ended up in slavery. Emanuel was doubtful my plan would work, but he was willing to try. So, we loaded up our vehicles and drove to another slum.

It would be simple, easy compared to staring down a couple of brick kiln slavers. Surely, the people in the slums were eager for their children to escape such a dark fate.

The people of the slum lived in garbage. Their children roamed the streets covered in filth, and their homes were nothing but cardboard, tin, or blankets hung in tatters across a crude frame. Arriving with our usual security detail, we walked around seeking a family willing to go with us. It was hot, crowded, and calamitous with the cries of beggars, the moans of the afflicted, and the sonorous strains of a Pakistani song being played somewhere in the network of entwined hovels. Human waste mingled with rotting vegetation, forming an odious smell I knew all too well in this country—despair. I took still shots for the website while shaking my head. *There is no way to fully capture this experience in photographs or videos.*

Emanuel, in compliance with my plan, asked different individuals if they wanted to come with us to live in a better place, one with clean water, clothing, medicine, school for their children, and decent food. I wondered how we would manage the onslaught of desperate souls rushing to our van as news of this offer rippled through the slum, but to my shock, nobody moved. They only asked for food.

Mercifully holding back a biting *"I told you so,"* Emanuel instead used this as a teachable moment for this firebrand American. "Dad, the slum is all these people have ever known. They are street smart. They are proud of their survival skills. They are a tight community. Their friends are here, their relatives. They can't see beyond this. They don't want to go."

I absorbed his words. These slum dwellers had found the one treasure that this hell-hole existence afforded—the community of souls.

One emaciated little girl followed us around while putting her fingers to her mouth—the universal sign for hunger. As I reached into my backpack for a power bar, Emanuel exclaimed, "Oh my God."

"What's wrong, Emanuel?"

"Dad, this little girl is sold to local men for sex."

"This little kid? How do you know?"

"You see that gold nose ring? It means she is a prostitute."

"But she's so young!"

"Dad," said Emanuel sadly. "The rape of Christian girls is so common. The desperate families send their girls out to prostitution. Even the mayor pays for virgins to rape."

That's all I needed to hear.

"Okay, we're getting her and her family out of here. Now!" I said with a little more emphasis than I intended.

We followed the little girl back to her shack, and Emanuel made inquiries to find her family. We found out her name was Shabnam, that she was twelve years old, and she was sold nightly. I was ready to tear this slum apart to find the parents who allowed this to happen to their daughter, but Emanuel was more pragmatic. Eventually, his inquiries brought us a message from the girl's parents through intermediaries.

"Dad, they will come with us, but not until tomorrow."

"Okay, good. We'll bring a truckload of rice and distribute it. Maybe some others will follow their example."

"Okay, let's go, Dad. It is too dangerous to be here for long. There are radicals watching from over there."

He motioned across the field to the busy street jammed with cars. I couldn't see anybody, but I trusted his judgment—it had saved my life many times.

We got back into the van and withdrew from the area. One of the security team members looked at me like: *"What did you just get us into?"*

The next morning, true to my amended plan, we loaded up the truck and drove back to the slum. Several of the security guys had spent the previous evening trying to convince the girl's suddenly resistant family to let us take them out. Making things worse, Shabnam kept running away and they couldn't find her. As we arrived with fifty-pound bags of rice, people began pushing and shoving to reach us. The flies were so bad we didn't dare breathe through our mouths. Everything we touched was dirty. Soon we were part of the filth.

One old lady got knocked down by a man who snatched her rice and ran off. In the midst of the chaos, Shabnam suddenly appeared with her fingers to her mouth. I gave her a bag, thinking we could follow her home and get her to come with us. The thought of this little girl being pimped out every night by grown men tore at me. From the dirt road running through the slum, I watched the frail Shabnam disappear carrying the fifty-pound rice bag on her head like it was nothing. I told one of the security guys which way she went, and he navigated through the crowd looking for her. He came back saying he could not find her.

Arriving back at our base of operations, we held our customary debrief. We talked for some time about the realities of actually rescuing children from the slums before they were taken or sold. We confronted the hard fact that because these slum inhabitants were streetwise and hardened, they were also resistant to our overtures of rescue.

After a while, the security guys returned with the family but not the girl. Even though they implored her to take this great opportunity, she still ran off. The mother and father had come, as well as some of their other children. I was devastated that Shabnam had refused. She was so young to be on her own among these lust-thirsty devils. Later, Emanuel came to me and said the mother was being difficult, making all kinds of demands.

"Doesn't she realize that we will help her family make a new life and that she will not live in the slums anymore?"

Emanuel looked sad. "Dad, I don't think these people are grateful. Maybe we should think of another way to do this."

I could see he was frustrated.

"Okay, I thought this would work. We'll rethink things. Did your team have any success finding Shabnam?"

"I'll check," he said, pulling out his phone. In a minute, he exclaimed, "Dad, yes! They are taking her to where we are settling the family."

"Emanuel, if the parents are this difficult, what's to stop them from selling her again? Maybe we should place her with another family."

"Okay, Dad, I will check on this."

"I am sorry this was so difficult. I just wanted to rescue them before they were enslaved."

"Yes, Dad, it was a good idea. Maybe we will try again sometime."

We were on a learning curve. We had no one to follow, no blueprints detailing how to do this. We made mistakes and we learned; we grew from both the victories and the failures. In the end—which really never came—we knew we had made an impact . . . one soul at a time.

Children labor to make mud for bricks.

19

An Adversarial Advocate

IT WAS TIME TO HEAD OUT for another rescue at a brick kiln—something at which we were growing more proficient. As usual, we were well armed. *Blessed are the meek.*
. . .

We loaded up the van with Tom in the front and Chris and I in the back. Emanuel drove and the security team followed in a second vehicle. Emanuel had heard that this brick kiln owner was particularly brutal. It was a two-hour drive ending in a narrow, winding dirt path leading to the brick kiln. We saw the owner sitting in a cabana, fanning himself in the heat as the field of slaves toiled under the blistering sun. We didn't pause to ask for permission, we just drove through the brick piles to where the slaves were working.

Walking around the brickfield, we picked two families who seemed in the worst shape. As we walked these families out, I noticed the father was hunched over and his toes were twisted. Emanuel explained, "Dad, this man from his youth had to walk in the mud and mix the straw and mud with his feet."

The man's wife had gnarled hands from working the brick forms. I glanced at Tom and Chris. Tom's head was on a swivel, always looking to place himself strategically for security—exactly the training I valued.

With the broken families in tow, Emanuel, Tom, Chris, and I trekked over to the cabana to start negotiations. Tom continued to survey the surroundings. Chris made obvious motions with his video camera and Emanuel translated.

"We were here to take people to freedom," I said to the owner with as much ferocity as I could muster. Emanuel translated.

The owner smiled back at me through gold framed glasses set off against his bronze skin. Twirling the ends of his exaggerated mustache with long, narrow fingers, he was the picture of serenity. For all I knew, he could have been a pianist preparing to perform the Rachmaninov no. 2. In a sense, that's exactly what he was doing.

"Something to drink?" he asked casually, motioning toward the bottle and empty glasses set there by a servant.

I was a little taken aback. I'd just fired off one of my best lines, and this guy wanted to buy the world a Coke?

"We didn't come here to drink," I said hotly. "We represent justice and health for children. We have been all over this nation. I am a Christian, and these Christians are my people."

My gaze left no question regarding my intentions.

"No, these are our people," said the owner nonchalantly as he waved his hands, turned away from the video camera, and looked off into the distance.

"No, they are Christians, so they are my people," I replied tersely. "We are recording this for publication. Do you want your face on the air? An advocate—the enslaver of people?"

"They are ours!" he fired back, suddenly alert, the façade gone, the lawyer rising to defend his territory.

Ah . . . struck a nerve, did I?

At the sound of his fury, a collective shudder rippled through the families standing with us. A few words from Emanuel calmed them enough to keep them from bolting back to the brickfields.

"Well, whatever you think they are, they are about to be free, so you can—"

I was about to say, "—take your arrogance and die!" but Emanuel's hand on my arm reminded me of the mission. We were there to free slaves, not kill the master, though the latter would have been sweetly satisfying in the interim.

"You cannot take them! They are mine! Get out or I will call the police!" he demanded.

Glancing over my left shoulder, I saw the van surrounded by other slaves slipping between seats as the team guided them. *Good. Keep him arguing.*

"You know the law," I said, wishing it were so.

"Yes I do. This is my country!" he exploded. "You have no rights here. It is God-ordained that we have slaves. Who are you, anyway? I should have you killed. All of you! I think I will!"

"We are taking them away," I said matter-of-factly. "Here is your payment."

Emanuel threw a small amount of cash on the owner's desk. The sum was symbolic; it would not even buy him a good meal, judging by how this guy lived.

Playing my best card, I turned my back on the gasping owner and calmly led our team and the slaves to the nearly filled van. Tom exchanged glances with the security team, indicating we were nearing our departure point.

As on other rescues, women were pushing their children into the van and begging us to take them. It was a scene that never failed to rip my heart—a mother's love until her dying breath. From his shaded vantage point, I knew the owner could not see the van, nor was he likely to follow us. It would have been . . . undignified. He'd been outmanned, and he knew it. To protest further would cause him to lose face—and we were recording this for worldwide distribution.

Once everyone was safely inside the van, we drove these beautiful people to freedom. At the compound, Chris filmed the van pulling in as I stood by the door to greet these liberated souls. Tom counted heads as they exited. "That's fifteen, twenty-four, thirty, forty, and the last one . . . forty-seven!"

We laughed—forty-seven children and adults climbing out of a fifteen-passenger van. This could have been a clown car at the circus if it wasn't so tragic. Forty-seven souls taken to freedom. We fed them, then asked questions.

"How long have you been a slave?" I asked an old man.

"My whole life," he said quietly, his head down, a permanent condition with lifelong slaves. "I was born there. My mother was a slave."

"Do you know where your relatives are?"

"Maybe in a village I have heard about?"

"Would you like to go there? Do you know the name of it?"

"I think I can remember."

"Okay, we can help you go there if you'd like."

"Yes, but what will I do now?"

"We will help you get a job or set up a small business if you would like."

"Yes, I would like that."

I thought of Jesus when he asked the blind man if he really wanted to be healed. Begging was a respected profession in his day. If sight was restored, the man would have to learn something new—not as easy as it sounds. Indeed, as bad as slavery was, it was all these slaves knew. In impoverished communities, victims cannot see beyond their own agonizing reality. The thought of change is overwhelming and can be more frightening than their abuse.

Yet the desire for freedom burns strong in many. Runaway slaves were showing up at our headquarters daily—broken people, crushed mentally and physically. A woman, her infant daughter, and her husband arrived at our door one day. In a faltering voice, she pleaded with us. She was beaten every day, and her father who was still at the brick kiln, would be beaten or killed if she did not return or pay their debt. We assured her we would get her father, they would be free, and no one would hurt them. The infant was sickly. The woman's husband was quiet as she spoke; he was also frail. When he finally spoke, he could barely be heard. His right arm was crippled, possibly broken. We had a doctor treat them.

Orphan Girls

The next morning, Emanuel said, "Dad, the slave owners know about you. They know what you are doing here.

They hate you. You are taking away their profits. They want you gone."

"Fine, Emanuel. Tell them to free their slaves and I'll leave."

"Dad, I wish it worked that way."

"I do too, Emanuel. Someday it will. We will see it."

"I see now, Dad."

I was glad to hear that our reputation as liberators was growing among the owners. It meant it was also growing among the slaves.

Later that day, we met with twenty local men who worked with Emanuel and helped us with our mission. We discussed some basic expectations, and I encouraged them to stay in the fight. We then prayed together and I gave them a basic stipend. These men, along with many other men and women, were vital to our success, as they were the ones who led us to the places where we rescue slaves. They put their lives in danger every day and were beaten by slave owners if they were caught near the slaves, ministering to their needs.

During our meeting we received intel that some orphaned girls needed immediate rescue. A local man had contacted Emanuel to tell him of their plight. We immediately loaded up our convoy and headed out on this unplanned rescue.

Of all we rescue—men and women, boys and girls—it is the orphans who are at the greatest risk, and of this group, girls stand to suffer a far worse fate.

These girls were forced to fend for themselves, fighting to survive. The longer they were unprotected, the more danger they faced. It was only a matter of time until they were sold to brothels, made sexual slaves, became pregnant, and were discarded or died from STDs.

We had learned early on that every brick kiln is different. The layout is different, the dynamics are different, the owners react differently, even the slaves are different. This one was odd. We had to walk far from our van, over dirt mounds and trails, to reach the working slaves. Tactically speaking, this was not ideal. Worse, we saw mostly adults; very few children.

Emanuel spoke to some slaves and then said, "Dad, we need to go somewhere else. Nobody knows where these girls are."

Disappointed, we trekked back to our car, continuing to ask various slaves as we went. "Where are the children?"

"They are gone," they replied, not daring to look at us.

As the team entered the vans, however, several slaves approached Emanuel's window. After a few minutes of discussion, they said they knew where the orphan girls were working. We got back out and walked past several brick buildings—simple structures that housed slaves in conditions a rat would despise. Behind one building were some girls shoveling dirt out of a hillside. We had found the orphans we'd been looking for.

Emanuel spoke to them, asking if they would like to be free and go to school. He assured them we were not taking them to be slaves again. Upon hearing his words, the youngest of the girls who looked to be about ten years old, broke into a smile. Another said she had been praying the day before to be freed from slavery. There was no doubt these girls had all been abused physically, mentally, and sexually. They led us to another family: a mom with two boys and a girl. The owner had beaten the father to death—something that happens often. When we told the mom we were taking them to freedom, she broke into tears and threw down the shovel.

We walked the slaves up to the owner's porch. Instead of one owner, however, there were several. I was starting to feel outnumbered. Emanuel identified the men as wealthy radicals by the way they dressed.

"Oh, these are very bad men. Please Dad, do not say these Christians are your people. They will become very angry, and they have a lot of weapons."

"Okay, stay close guys," I said, turning to Tom and Chris. "Emanuel, we are ready."

We entered the roofed porch where seven men were seated and waiting for us. One was the owner—his icy arrogance gave him away. I thought of the poem Ozymandias, by Percy Bysshe Shelly:

. . . Half sunk, a shattered visage lies, whose frown
And wrinkled lip, and sneer of cold command,
Tell that its sculptor well those passions read . . .

Another was obviously a radical leader based on how he dressed and the colors he displayed. The rest were merely followers, not an immediate threat but could be trouble if things escalated.

My team, the owner, and the radical team sat in a circle. Mr. Radical Leader was to my right. Tom was to my left. Chris, with the all-seeing video camera, sat across from me and next to Emanuel. I told the owners who we were— journalists and humanitarians who were rescuing children and filming a documentary for worldwide distribution. The lead slimeball smirked at the slaves—they were clearly terrified to be in the presence of their owners—and then quickly recovered his demeanor.

"Tea for you? Or Coke?" he asked with ritual politeness.

"No, we are full from lunch," I said, rubbing my empty stomach.

"It is our custom for you to have tea with us."

I wanted to say, "It is my custom to punch your face," but a frown from Emanuel calmed me down.

"Thank you for asking," I replied. "We are part of a humanitarian mission. We are here to take these slaves to get medical care. They are badly hurt and need help. Surely an organization as large as yours cannot care for everyone. We are taking these families with us."

"What? You are trying to destroy our business. These people are highly trained. We depend on them. How can we compete with you taking our best workers?"

I let my eyes do the talking as I bored a hole through the back of his skull. *Destroy your business? Sure, us taking two injured families out of the hundreds you own will destroy you. In fact, I hope it does.*

"We are here to help people," I said with more force. "To evaluate the health needs of children and to help them have a new life."

I noticed Emanuel's voice trembling as he translated. It was unusual to see him this nervous. Apparently, this situation was worse than I realized. It dawned on me that with his connections throughout the Taliban, the lead owner could make a call and we would be swarmed by militants in minutes.

"Of course. Yes, this is a good thing, especially for the children," the leader said, smiling and clearly not feeling a word of it.

"How long have you owned this brick kiln?" I asked in the face of his sarcasm.

"Thirty years I have owned it. I have done well, have I not?"

I nodded, wondering how a human being can put money over the lives of his fellow men. They see slaves as commodities to be traded, abused and extinguished as they wish. It happens every day. Only a sociopathic society could allow a slave trade like this to flourish. My mind burned with arrows to hurl at these creatures.

How many children have you killed here?

How many girls have you raped?

How many slaves have you personally beaten to death?

How long can you live with my hands around your—

"I'm glad you see things our way," Emanuel said with a side glance to me.

The radical leader glanced at his phone. We were only fifteen feet from the road, easy access to an angry horde. To my shock, I saw several of his kind wearing similar radical garb, walking down the road towards us. Tom saw them too. My hand slid down to my holstered knife. Tom tensed. Every owner's eyes followed my movement. To my surprise, however, the walking radicals peered at us but kept going. Chris continued filming, and the owners grew restless.

As Emanuel engaged the owner directly in Urdu, Mr. Radical grew agitated. This was the danger zone, the moment where they acquiesce or they attack. My gut told me all hell was about to break loose.

"I think it's time to go," Tom whispered quietly, his eyes scanning the horizon.

Before we could retreat, however, Mr. Radical abruptly stood and left without a word. *Was he gathering some of his men?*

To my astonished relief, he returned quickly, with his assistant following and carrying the debt book. In the ensuing discussion, they determined what these families owed—it was a debt that could not be repaid without outside intervention. Emanuel reviewed the numbers, bartered a little, and quickly satisfied the debt by giving them over half of what they asked for. It was not a large amount, but even a dollar is too much for the lives of human beings. This largess was unheard of in our negotiations. Normally, we settled for pennies on the dollar. But nothing about this rescue was normal. We were out-manned and possibly outgunned. Emanuel explained later that it was too dangerous to do anything else. We were in a very bad area, and they could have ambushed us in an instant—video camera be damned.

With our business concluded, Emanuel and I stood up in front of the lead owner while everyone else moved out of the covered porch area. I was angry that these innocent Christians had been abused, raped, tortured, and killed at the whims of these monsters. Everything in me—and I'm sure of the team—wanted to eliminate these radicals. But somehow, igniting World War III did not seem as good an idea as getting the hell out of there with our initial objective intact.

The two families quickly filed into the van, along with the orphan girls and apparently several other stowaways as well. We left quickly before their absence was noticed. At Emanuel's house, we spoke with the rescued people about plans for homes, school, businesses, and more. They were elated, saying they have always wanted to be free, to earn a living and have a home. To live in peace.

The next day was a hot one. Taking a rest from life-altering rescues, we drove to a far-away village to visit a rescued family and see how they were doing after several days of freedom. We decided to set up the man with a donkey and cart for a fruit stand. We found that when we give a business to freed slaves, they work very hard to make it successful. We train them in how to run the business, and they achieve a high degree of success.

When we arrived, other people began to gather. They had heard that the men who set slaves free were here. After a brief conversation with the freed slaves and seeing that they were okay, we started driving down the narrow streets again. Hundreds of people gathered around us. Emanuel stopped and rolled down his window to speak with an elderly woman who begged for her life to be spared from the brick kiln. So many were begging for freedom.

Emanuel listened to her story, and said we needed to find a family who has eleven children. The mother thinks the slave owner is going to sell them to other kilns. We drove through the village, parked the car, and found the small house of the family who needed to be rescued. We listened to their story, and I was convinced.

"Emanuel, we need to load them into the van and make them disappear."

He agreed and called for an additional van. As we walked out, a huge crowd surrounded us. The old woman from before ran to my side begging for freedom. All I could do was look at her—there are so many wanting freedom. Emanuel left the local contact behind to wait on the van for the thirteen family members and at my request, the old woman.

When the van arrived at the compound, we were expecting thirteen people but twenty-three spilled out. We learned that others had jumped in as the van was getting ready to leave. We watched with joy as the rescued families devoured hot food, drank fresh water, and smiled. A few laughed. One woman laid down and slept. She looked worn out and defeated. It was probably the first real sleep she'd had in years. One man got up slowly, his legs and body stiff. He walked over to us and started to talk. I asked for someone to translate. He said they had prayed for so long for freedom, and thanked me for freeing his family. He told me I had saved the lives of his children, and maybe they can learn in school and be healthy.

We all smiled with him. Freedom that day was real for him, his family, and the others. Indeed, it was real for all of us.

Two children working hard to please the cruel slave master.

20

Valentine's Day Ambush

"DAD, WE ARE GOING TO A MORE DANGEROUS AREA," Emanuel called out. "It is more Taliban. There are many slaves there, and many sick children. The police have cleared us to go. We must go now."

I knew it was Valentine's Day back home. What better way to honor the martyred priest who assisted Christian couples than to free modern Christian slaves?

The team was ready, gear was packed. We had been waiting hours for the go ahead. Tom, Rick, Jon, Aaron, and I would head out while my wife, Aricka, would stay at the compound to work with some of the rescued children. I grabbed the GPS tracker and switched it on. The support staff back home would see our movements, and should anything happen—if we were ambushed or kidnapped—one of us would try to push the red button. Then the rescue operation would begin. Hopefully a rescue mission, not a recovery mission.

I have always hated navigating through the city. The air tastes bitter from smog. The traffic is thick, and we have to pass through Taliban-held areas. A two-lane road typically has five lanes of cars, donkey carts, rickshaws, motorbikes, and the occasional camel. It would be easy to get trapped at intersections.

Tom was in the front, an AK-47 at his feet. The rest of us had 9mm pistols hidden on our persons or in a quick-retrieve pocket in a backpack. Not far from our home base, the security guys in the front car stopped and got out. There was a large duffle bag left along the road. The security guys walked around it, then called back to Emanuel. He got out, walked a short way toward the guards, then returned. The guards moved the bag out of the way and Emanuel turned the car down a narrow alley and maneuvered through very rough sections of the streets. We learned later this was an IED meant for my team, and it blew ten minutes after we passed it. Thank God for cheap timers!

It took two hours to get to the edge of the town where we wanted to do the rescues. Emanuel received a phone call. The conversation was quite animated. He hung up and his voice was strained. "Dad, we need to go to a different place now. The area where we were going is not safe. Somehow, they found out we were nearby and set an ambush for us. There are many men with guns."

"Okay, I am glad we were warned. Let's go to another brick kiln. Please thank whoever that was for me."

Emanuel was on the phone, again, talking with his security team and our other team members who were in the two cars ahead of us. Tom, Aaron, and I were in the car with Emanuel. Aaron, our videographer, stayed busy getting B-roll (filler footage to add into the final video). A few miles into our drive, the cars turned onto a different road. A half-hour later we arrived at another dangerous village. We pulled off the dirt road and descended into a brick kiln area, evident by the ever-present red dust rising up from the turning tires. We drove past the main building and to the edge of where the bricks were formed.

Aaron was quick to get out and get the video camera ready as the security guys spread out. Tom and I exchanged glances, both of us realizing this was a place where a crap storm could start quickly. Tom, Rick, and Jon—all well-trained guys—formed a perimeter around us. I followed Emanuel, and we were joined by a few other men I did not recognize, most likely Emanuel's contacts. Everything was moving in slow motion. I walked casually as a growing crowd watched from the road. There was no sense in projecting anything but peace. Aaron was walking and filming to my right. He had set me up with a wireless mic prior to leaving our compound, so I narrated what was taking place.

"This is a high alert area, and we are walking to the back to identify slaves we plan to set free."

Over my shoulder, I saw traffic piling up with onlookers. This was not good at all. Our safe exposure time in this more radical area was measured in seconds.

After a few minutes of walking, we arrived where two families were waiting. The father and mother looked confused. The woman held a metal brick form, and the father picked up his little girl. Several young girls were working hard, putting the bricks onto neat piles, their hands caked with red mud. Even though they are slave children, they had outfits of blue, green, red, and even purple. One young girl wore a blue winter jacket with the hood up even though the day was brutally hot. All the children were barefoot. Each appeared gaunt, with looks of absolute defeat. "The walking dead" is the only way I can describe the adults. Gaunt cheeks, dirty hair, thin bodies, and clothing covered in red dirt, their faces etched by hardship and hunger.

Emanuel was talking with a woman who was holding a baby. Speaking to the camera, I intoned: "This child will never know what it is like to be a slave—this beautiful, beautiful baby—because we will rescue this family."

Tom, ever vigilant, gave me the eye. He was anxious to get moving. We were in deep danger, but the price for not getting these enslaved people out was that they would suffer in ways most people cannot imagine.

Gathering the slaves together, I examined the fear in their eyes. *What are they thinking? What have they seen? Endured? What do they know but can never convey about real suffering?*

I will never fully understand what it is like to have been born into slavery. Not a day of life where these slaves have been free, not a day where they are not subjugated and abused, not a day where they have had health care, proper nutrition, or in most cases, clean water. Not a single day of education. Most do not know anything about the world, many do not know where they came from, and many have not been able to identify other countries— or sometimes even their own. There is not much for slaves beyond the day-to-day life of labor, abuse, and being traded and treated like animals. As I looked at these two families with their precious children, I couldn't bear the idea of them living like this for one more day.

The team and I explained to the families that we were going to make them free. I led them out as the team took strategic positions. The children grabbed our hands, knowing something momentous was happening.

"Okay, let's get moving. There are too many people gathering by the road."

As we headed to the owner's compound, a man approached Emanuel from the opposite direction and walked alongside him while I continued to work. The man was slight in build, dressed in all white. He had the typical mustache and dark-rimmed glasses of the upper class.

After a minute of banter, Emanuel came for me.

"Dad, that was the owner. He's an advocate," said Emanuel.

"Are you saying he's a lawyer?" I asked.

"Yes, he's a lawyer as well as the brick kiln's owner."

"Do you think he'll be a problem?"

"I don't know," Emanuel said, lowering his voice.

We entered the brick porch area of the owner's building and waited for the owner to return with his partner.

"So, you are the owner here?" I asked.

"We want to end slavery," Emanuel offered.

"We are taking these families to freedom," exclaimed Emanuel with an air of authority. "You are a man of the law. You know that no children under the age of fourteen are allowed to work."

"You cannot take them," came the predictable response. "They have many debts to me, and besides, these people do not work for me."

I turned to the camera: "They do not want us to take their people. They are being dishonest."

The crowd gathering at the road effectively blocked off any chance of exiting.

"Tom, this is a red alert area," I said for the benefit of the camera.

"Yes, I know," Tom replied tensely.

Tom was about fifteen feet from where Emanuel and I were arguing with the owner. Tom's back was to a brick wall and his hand was in his pack, which he had swung around to the front. He had his hand on a weapon. I looked over and both Jon and Rick were positioned to see the road as well as the gathering crowd. They could also see me and the growing crowd of slaves that were pressing in to hear what was happening. Good positioning. It was growing very tense as the slave owner was arguing with Emanuel. I interjected a few times, but they couldn't hear me in the growing commotion. Aaron stayed focused on the video, but we all knew this was a bad situation. I was about to call for departure but the owner relented and brought out his books to show what the debts were. I do not like to ever give money in these situations, but I negotiated the debt down to two cents on the dollar. Emanuel gave the families the money, and they paid off their debts. The owner was beyond furious.

"Emanuel, we have to go NOW!"

"Yes, yes, let's go!"

"Emanuel, this is a bad situation." Someone, perhaps Rick, had ordered Emanuel's security guys to go make a path in the road. These guys do not mess around. I have seen them fire shots in the air to part a crowd, and in one case, shoot a guy who was causing problems where we were staying.

At the same time this was happening, Emanuel was still arguing with the owners, and I piped in that we were taking these people. It was not translated, as there was so much commotion. Emanuel whirled around and spoke to the families, and they were taken to the van. It looked as if there were twelve people, then a few others snuck in.

We loaded up and the cars pulled up to the road, made a left turn through the crowd, drove about fifty meters, and turned left into another kiln.

"What are we doing Emanuel? We need to get out of this area now!"

"Dad, there are many slaves here who need rescuing."

We all jumped out and I immediately started talking to the video camera, walking quickly, explaining what we were doing. We walked a short way and saw two orphan slave children. Emanuel began talking to them, telling them they were going to be free and they'd never have to touch a brick again. These beautiful children were dressed in ragged clothing and looked confused at first. But it all changed in a single, dramatic moment! Understanding that they were about to be freed, the little boy and girl raised bricks and threw them down hard enough to smash them. Victory for these kids! The little boy was so dirty that red mud caked his hair, but all I saw was a beautiful kid. His sister looked the same, with red mud caked on her feet and hands. She looked up at me with the slightest of smiles. My heart melted. I put my hand on their heads and told them, although they did not understand my words, that we were taking them out of here. Somehow children always know to smile for a camera, and these kids were no different. It was beautiful.

We began to walk towards the van where Tom, Rick, and Jon had assembled. The crowd was growing, people were shouting, "Make us free! Take us with you!"

We were working as fast as we could to get the slaves inside the van. Rick said, "There are too many people! We can't shut the doors!" It was overwhelming. I appreciated Tom's vigilance. Rick and Jon, tough as nails, were always quiet, doing their jobs to secure the perimeter along with Emanuel's team. But now we needed to mobilize; we had been in the area too long. One phone call could bring armed radicals who were in abundance in this region.

I approached the van and saw that two men were half in and half out because the van was packed full, but there was no way we could leave like that. These people were beyond desperate for freedom. I looked through the dirty rear window, and there looked to be forty people crammed into the fifteen-passenger, very overloaded van. Wow, the big challenge now was how to close the door. The security team was spread out, and I heard one of my team members say, "Let's get the heck out of here." The owner was not around, so we got the people jammed in and all pulled out.

As we drove down the highway, I marveled at how many people were jammed in the van, knowing they would slowly realize they were free. We pulled alongside the van, waved, and saw many smiling faces. This was an awesome moment! Soon they would be getting new clothes, a hot meal, showers, and then a long ride to their new home in a distant village. Life was good and getting better.

Used as a living billboard, this little girl was dressed up and made to stand by the building to attract men to a brothel. She was rescued.

21

Eighty Slaves and Poison

IN 2015, MY WIFE JOINED ME and my team on a rescue mission in Pakistan. During the rescue, Aricka picked up a baby and noticed the red and runny eyes—pink eye. A little later, Aricka had it too.

The rescue freed a large number of slaves. At the compound, Aricka interviewed a teenage girl, fourteen at the most. This beautiful child, enslaved in a brick kiln her entire life, told Aricka how she labored all day, was beaten often, and attended school in the evening.

"How could you get away from the owner to attend school?" Aricka asked.

The girl looked to the ground and was quiet.

"What's the matter?" asked Aricka.

"The owner often leaves in the afternoon," the girl said, not looking up. "And when I can, I ask the guard to let me leave. He makes me give him sex and then I can go to school for the evening."

Raw emotion covered Aricka's face. She continued to ask a few more questions, but we understood. Aricka walked away to compose herself.

Later in the day, we were scheduled to drive an hour and a half to a village where a slave couple was executed for burning pages of a sacred document. They were given a pile of trash to burn, and pages from the document were in the bag. The couple could not read, and could not have known what was in the pile. A villager positioned nearby claimed to see it and raised the alarm in the village. The enraged villagers rushed to the kiln, grabbed the couple, and dragged them over to the furnace vents—large holes atop the kiln—where they were burned alive.

We had come to meet with some government officials about the atrocity, make a public statement, and record everything on video for distribution.

During this time, Aricka's eyes worsened and were nearly swollen shut, yet she endured it stoically. She told me, through grim determination, that the slaves endure things like pink eye with no relief or medical help, so she could endure it too.

We drove back to the compound in silence and stopped at a street pharmacy where we got pink eye medicine for a dollar. One dollar. A slave owner who becomes filthy rich cannot spend a dollar to heal a slave.

Bastards, all of them.

An Impromptu Rescue

We were on our way to a slave camp that had hundreds of slaves. Our convoy of security, team members, and empty vans for rescued slaves drove two hours to reach the brick kiln. On the way, we passed a large factory surrounded by high fences with barbed wire. Emanuel knew a person who worked there.

"Dad, the children are chained to machines for their whole life. They live and die there," Emanuel struggled to say. "Dad, a slave boy takes a bucket to them so they can relieve themselves, others take them handfuls of rice and water every day, but the slave children never leave the machines . . . many, many die there."

He said there were hundreds of slaves inside. His description of the conditions stilled the atmosphere in the car. Aricka, my wife, shook her head in disbelief. I looked out the rear window at the quickly disappearing factory. Inside, children were suffering unspeakable horrors and there was nothing I could do about it. These factories were impossible for our team to infiltrate.

We journeyed on in silence and focused on the task at hand. We eventually pulled off the main road onto a secondary road where we drove for fifteen minutes. The sky was clear and the heat was intensifying. We drove past water buffalo, field workers (most likely slaves), and through a small village. After another five minutes on a dirt road, we arrived at a large brick kiln.

As we pulled in, we noticed the main building to our right, with secondary buildings to the left. We did not see any owners sitting under the porch area. Our convoy drove down a dirt lane heading towards the brick kiln area. We took a sharp left turn onto an open dirt area and parked. The area was surrounded by ten-foot-high dirt ridges that separated the areas of the fields where the slaves worked. Tom ascended the ridge facing north and surveyed the area. There were slaves working as far as he could see.

The rest of the team stood around the vehicles waiting for Emanuel to tell us where to go. He had gone for a short walk with his local contact and soon returned in a hurry. "Dad, the owner is not here. What do you want to do?" He could have predicted my answer.

"Let's take as many slaves as we can before he returns!"

"I don't know, Dad. It may be too dangerous."

"Everything we do is dangerous, Emanuel."

Rick spoke up in the background. "Let's just do it and get out of here."

"What do the rest of you think?" I asked the team.

"Let's get the vehicles filled up and go," was the consensus.

Emanuel nodded in agreement, reached for his phone and called in some rickshaws and another van. He then told his men to start gathering up slaves. There were several hundred slaves there; I wasn't sure how he was picking the ones to take. Slaves—mostly men—were lining up on a small ridge to the west, curious about what we were doing.

The rickshaws and another van arrived. Emanuel's security team gathered the slave children and families and were stuffing them into vehicles. As near as I could estimate, we had eighty to ninety slaves crammed together. Aricka, Tom, and I got into Emanuel's car and the convoy rolled out of the brickfield in record time. Ever wary, Tom held the AK-47 in his lap and I kept my 9mm within a finger's reach. As we drove past the building near the road, a very tall slave was walking out onto the road. Emanuel asked if he wanted a ride. "No, I will walk to my freedom," he exclaimed. I am not sure how he would get to our compound, but he seemed resolute and brave.

A few frantic miles down the dirt road, Emanuel's phone buzzed.

"Dad, we are being followed."

I knew the security team was behind us, but we did not know who and how many vehicles were pursuing us. I turned around with my back against the driver's seat, rolled down the window and rested the 9mm on the ledge. Tom had his weapon up and ready. Everyone was tense until Emanuel got another call.

"We're okay. The security team dealt with it."

I was not sure what that meant, but I didn't ask. We drove on. Once we reached the main highway, we slowed down to let the rescue vehicles pass. They were jam-packed with the smiling faces of newly freed children and adults. *I could live in this moment forever.*

Knowing these beautiful humans were free was ecstasy for me. As each vehicle drove by, our team cheered for joy. Aricka was beaming. However, we all knew that crap was about to hit the fan. We had taken over eighty slaves from a bad man in a Taliban-held area, in a country considered one of the most dangerous on the planet. The key now was to get the people back to base, get them food and showers, and make them disappear.

Life would not be easy for them in a country like Pakistan, where Christians are considered the lowest of humans. With our help, however, most of these people would stay free and be as successful as possible. A small number, however, would borrow money again from the brick kilns, or in the case of one family, run away from freedom and put themselves back in slavery. The fear of being found by the slave master drove them to return to the only life they'd known. A lifetime of psychological torment and manipulation had bound them mentally and emotionally to the control of a monster. Fortunately, ninety-nine percent of those we've rescued have remained free, and we did everything in our power to make it so.

It is vital for the people we rescued to not contact anyone after we set them up with a new life. One woman we had rescued the year before decided to call her aunt. What she did not know was her ex-slaver had beat up her aunt and ordered her to call him should she be contacted by the former slave. He found out where she and her family were and drove hours to get them. He was a member of the Pakistani Parliament and was very powerful. Emanuel found out where this family was taken and sent a few of his guys to take them back. They had been tortured—badly. The team got them out and took them to a new location. They learned a hard lesson and required many months of recovery. As far as I know, they are still free today.

We arrived back at the compound ahead of the rescue vehicles. When the fifteen-passenger vans pulled in, Aricka and I, along with the team, walked over to greet them. With Aaron on the video camera, we welcomed each person as they pried themselves from the van. Old, very old, young, very young—all free today. We gathered them together and talked about freedom and what was to come for them. An old man started to dance, and everyone broke into a song about freedom.

Amidst this celebration, evidence of their abuse and animal-like living conditions were apparent. Dirt clung to their feet; only a few had sandals. They wore dirty, ripped clothes. Children had mud caked on their hands; one girl had dirt caked up her legs. One man was missing fingers. Several young girls had nose rings signifying they were the sexual property of the owner. Several older women had gnarled feet from a lifetime of walking on brick molds. There was a man with scars on the side of his face and top of his head, and a little girl had red dirt caked in her hair. An older man had a scar across his left eye, and an old woman could not stand up straight. As I realized how much these people had suffered and were now free, tears flooded my eyes.

Aricka held a baby; both were smiling broadly. That child would never know a life of slavery.

A Parting Gift

On the day we were to fly home, Emanuel took our team to a nice hotel for dinner. I had been there several times, and it had several layers of security to get in. Some of the food was a mystery, but everything looks good when you're famished. This area of the restaurant was in a court-yard, and from our table we could see the sky. Everyone was tired and talk was minimal. We looked forward to our flight.

We placed our orders and waited in silence. When the waiter delivered our food, I noticed he kept looking back over his shoulder at me as he walked away. I should have been more alert to this strange behavior, but exhaustion had set in, and I was not at my best.

During the two-hour trip to the airport, I felt odd. I can't describe it, but something was going on. I fell asleep on the plane. According to Aricka, I woke up mid-flight completely disoriented, stood up, and started going through the overhead bin trying to find medicine. She helped me calm down, and I ended up sleeping fitfully the rest of the flight.

At home I developed severe itching. It felt like a thousand fire ants biting me. I met with the doctor several times, and after getting no answers for weeks, he sent me to the Cleveland Clinic where a neurologist told me I was experiencing a kind of neuropathy typically caused either by diabetes (which I did not have), toxins, or poison. The picture of the waiter walking away came to mind. Poison . . . again.

After some research, I discovered that my picture and Emanuel's picture had been circulated around the country—a contract was put on our lives.

It took a year and a half for the neuropathy to subside, to recover my strength, and for other issues to disappear. One of the strange effects was that if I started to sweat, my skin felt like fire. This went on for months. Finally, I told Aricka I was going to run and sweat—fire be damned. If slaves could endure the hellfire of a brick kiln, I could outrun whatever was tormenting me. The pain was excruciating as I jogged around our property in the muggy heat of a Pennsylvania summer, but I pushed through. After an hour of sweating, the pain had diminished, and recovery was in sight.

I stayed active during the eighteen months I was off. We continued to build our organization, sponsoring people on rescues throughout the Middle East. Dozens of children were rescued by courageous men and women who worked with us. As my health improved, we developed plans to travel to different nations and get back to rescuing slaves. Soon we traveled back across the pond, stronger, better organized, and more determined to bring the light of freedom to captives living in the darkness of slavery.

What the enemy meant for evil, God used for good.

PART III

Into the Brothels

22

G-man's Vision

By G-man

I AM G-MAN. I am forty-three, born in Asia in a high-class Hindu family where our family members used to worship hundreds of different gods and goddesses. My childhood was difficult, as my mom died three hours after giving birth to me and I grew up with the help of my grandmother. My father was a farmer and I had to work in the farm fields, planting, irrigating, and harvesting before and after the school time. I used to go to school, walking two hours every day. I have completed my school after years of hard work. As I grew older, I separated from my family due to major religious differences.

After that, difficulties in my life started again. No support from the family, no friends, went many days with an empty stomach, but I did not stop praying, even with tears in my eyes.

I started as a tutor to teach the small children and got some money for food and college fees. It ran for five years. After that, I completed my Bachelor's Degree and got a teaching job in a private school.

One day I was returning from the church, three people kidnapped me and I was taken to India. They asked me for $5,000 for setting me free but I did not have even a single dollar to give them. They threatened that if I did not give them money, they would kill me. They kept me in a dark room in a place where there was no village. Only some buffaloes and cows were there. The kidnappers told me if my wife would not call them for ransom, they would kill me the next day.

That night an old man came at midnight to see his animals with a torch light because there was no electricity. I was inside the room and locked from outside. I almost lost my hope to live but I was praying. I saw the small light and someone coming towards me. I thought they may be kidnappers, but I noticed the old man. I knocked on the door from inside but the old man thought I was a thief and came there to take his animal. He ran away to the village and called all the villagers to kill me, thinking I was there to steal his cattle. When the villagers saw me, one of the ladies knew me as a teacher of her grandson. She told all the villagers that I am a teacher in a school. I explained everything to the villagers; they set me free from the kidnappers.

Children in My Home Country

Many children are not going to school due to poverty.

Child slavery is often confused with child labor, but it is much worse. While child labor is harmful for children and hinders their education and development, child slavery occurs when a child's labor is exploited for someone else's gain.

Right after an earthquake in my country, millions of families lost their homes and family members, and thousands had to live on the streets. Hundreds of thousands of children in my country are deprived of education because the earthquakes destroyed their schools and created a great deal of poverty. One hundred thousand children under seventeen working in restaurants, the garment industry, brick industry, pulling rickshaws, etc. Many of them are misused for child labor and prostitution. In addition, hundreds of thousands of women lost their jobs, and most of them had to turn to prostitution for income.

Working with CRI

My wife and I have a great passion for helping women and children get out of rough circumstances and to get an education. In November 2017, we connected with Bruce Ladebu, the Founder/Director of Children's Rescue Initiative (CRI). He came to my country with his team and shared their mission and interest in rescuing children from trafficking and child labor. I thought it would be a great opportunity to work with Bruce and his team to save the children. From November 2017 until May 2018 we rescued nearly one hundred children from restaurants where they were used for child labor and prostitution. We rescued a family from the brick factory where they had been working in bound labor for two years. We are really thankful to God for the blessing of Bruce and his team.

After being rescued, we transported the children to safety. They were provided good food, clothes, and sent to school. Now they are all doing well physically and emotionally. We hope to rescue more children from brothels and human trafficking and continue to save lives. Here is the story of a girl we rescued.

Story of Nisha

My name is Nisha Magar. I am fifteen years old, and from a remote village. I used to go to school and I was in tenth grade, when three years ago a big flood in our village swept away our land and house. I lost my family in the flood and became homeless. There was no one to care for me. I visited a town to look for work with a lady from my village. The lady was involved in prostitution and earned money for her family. She encouraged me to get involved in sex work. I also thought I would have to do something for food, so I started to work in a small restaurant cleaning pots and sometimes going out for the sex work.

In the beginning I felt good because I was getting money from the customers, but later the owner of the restaurant took money from them and I had to sleep with them without being paid. I was upset, but it was my obligation to work there.

One day a man [G-man] came to the restaurant and asked for a cold drink. He asked me my name and about my family. I don't know why, but my eyes filled with tears. For the first time, someone had asked about me. The man came the next day, at the same time because it was mid-afternoon and I used to be somewhat free from work. He encouraged me to be strong and said he will do something to set me free from the sex work.

The next month he came with some other people and took me to his home. I was scared at the beginning, but slowly it became normal to be with this new family.

Now I am really happy, I am getting good food and clothes. I am going to school regularly. They are caring for me like my parents. They are teaching me how to pray and getting me involved in a Bible study with other children.

I have got a new life now. I am really thankful to the pastor in our local church too. He said some people from America are supporting us financially for our living and schooling. I am really thankful to them, too, because they have helped save my beautiful life.

Praise the Lord!

A rescued man was given a fruit stand to run to support his now freed family.

23

Breaking Down Brothels

2017

THE DYNAMICS OF A TEAM ARE EVERYTHING in the success of a mission. One wrong addition to a team can change the character of a trip and create turmoil among team members. This is why I try to vet all team members, and in an ideal situation, spend time training with them beforehand, not just to improve skills but to observe personalities and cohesiveness. This is why we require all prospective team members to attend CRI training. This week-long camp is an entrance into learning how we operate. It is an amazing time to get to know potential team members, to evaluate them, and to let them evaluate us.

In 2017, an impressive team was assembled, and we launched out on a rescue operation in a central Asian mountain environment. A longtime friend and security specialist wanted to join a rescue operation. His call sign was Yeti, named for his size. He was a highly trained, successful executive security specialist. Standing six feet, four inches tall, weighing 250 pounds of bone and pure muscle, bald, and sporting a goatee, he rarely had to argue to make his point. Perhaps that is why he was so pleasant. What's there to get uptight about? I was pleased to have him on the team.

Another resourceful component to that team was Catch Dog. He was a man of many talents. As an experienced combat specialist, he had seen more than his share of armed conflict in the service of our country. Fairly ripped and endowed with a great sense of humor, Catch Dog spoke with a soft southern accent and conveyed a gentle spirit. He was passionate about saving children from slavery. Having had enough combat experience in his life, he now longed to enter the world of rescuing children.

The third man on the team was Pipe Hitter. He was a private security contractor protecting oil and cargo ships sailing through the Suez Canal and off the coast of Somalia. He had heard our reputation and asked to join the team. We were excited to have him with us! Pipe Hitter looked the part for a hunter of bad people: white hair and a long white beard, with the attitude of a biker gang looking for the guy who kicked over their Harleys. He was built for battle, and he loved to regale us with stories of his adventures, laced with colorful expletives. He made the boring parts of travel fun.

Rounding out the group was Samurai, a photographer and videographer who joined the rescue team to help us record it for publication. He was tall and slender, a top athlete in school, and had a passion for capturing our stories for the world to see. In contrast to the commando team members, Samurai was a quiet guy and a natural listener—the quintessential gray man behind the lens. As I have said often in these stories, our most potent weapon in combating the craven cowards of the slave industry was the camera lens that threatened to expose them.

The main goal of this operation was to free children from brothels in Asia (although we also did some work in brick kilns). This was a change from our past trips where we focused primarily on freeing children from labor slavery in brick kilns and factories. There were many young girls trapped in sexual slavery in the region we were to visit. In fact, we learned that there was a major market for children there, with holding centers the size of warehouses where young girls and boys were held until they were shipped to other nations.

G-man was our local contact. I met him through a friend, and after many conversations, I decided he would be the guy we would work within this country. G-man grew up in the area and had a heart to rescue victims of slavery.

Once we landed in Asia, processed through customs and retrieved our luggage from the insanely unorganized baggage area, we exited the terminal and saw a sign being held up that said "BRUCE."

There was G-man, smiling and greeting us in his Asian accent. He looked us over, and we did the same to him. G-man was of average height for his country, his black hair was mixed with some gray, and his dark, intense eyes were edged in merriment. I was pleased to see he was professionally attired in slacks and a dress shirt. He had arranged a small SUV with a driver who took us to a bed and breakfast type of place. We settled in and went downstairs to get some food at a coffee shop. It was a place frequented by westerners, and the food was to our liking.

The first sign of trouble came through our conversation with G-man, who became somewhat argumentative as to actually being able to rescue children. I was agitated but understood his reluctance for conflict. It was a cultural thing, one of the factors that made this country a hotbed of slavery in plain view of the populace. He just needed a little . . . um, encouragement.

"G-man, we came halfway around the world, and you agreed to do this. Now you're saying we can't?"

"Bruce, it is too difficult. The traffickers are very organized. They are dangerous."

"G-man, we have been doing these rescues for years. We know how to do this. You take us where the children are, and we will show you how we do it."

"I do not think we can do this."

"You need to trust us. We will keep you safe."

"Okay," came his hesitant reply.

Yes, we had come to rescue children, but we had also come to train people like G-man.

We spent several days with G-man, studying the locales, assessing the dangers, and pouring over maps. By the third day we had a plan and were driving several hundred miles to a city known to be a hub for trafficking. The trip was challenging with seven guys in a tiny SUV traveling on narrow mountain roads. The SUV's tires skirted the crumbled edge of a narrow road cut into the side of a mountain. We were inches from a thousand-foot drop. Worse, Yeti and I were crammed into the rear seat, his knees jammed against my knees while we tried shifting slightly to keep from cramping and too much cuddling.

"Yeti, next trip, I'm bringing a hobbit," I said.

"Fine with me, Professor."

Hours upon hours we rode like this. Catch Dog slept through everything. Pipe Hitter got the front seat next to the driver, thanks to his car sickness. At the height of my sardine misery, a thought struck me. *Say . . . how does a pirate hunter who rode the high seas get carsick?*

High in the mountains, the views were incredible, even if the ride was torturous. With all the curves and sudden stops as cars and trucks vied for position on these shelf roads that were barely wide enough for one vehicle, rest was out of the question. Pushing the paradoxical physics out of my mind, I focused instead on the verdant valleys filled with terraced hillsides chiseled out of mountain sides over eons by farmers intent on growing splendid crops. Beautiful rivers flowed through valleys below and sparkled in sunlight. Ascending higher and higher, our view expanded for hundreds of miles. Hawks floated below us, as did clouds. Passing through timeless villages, I studied the buildings, realizing many were very old—possibly centuries old even. I thought of the lives, the generations, that had passed through these lands. Buildings erected with care by people long forgotten were now left to unseeing generations.

Cresting the final mountain range, we made the long, slow descent into a region of rusted factories, ominous brick kilns, polluted air, and dark enterprises. We eventually arrived at our destination—a decrepit motel in a dangerous border town. In contrast to the snow-capped mountains that had heralded our arrival, the town was flat and dirty, air thick with pollution, streets choked with chaotic traffic. The main thoroughfares were wide in the center of town, but the side streets were narrow and mostly dirt—until it rained. Ramshackle houses and apartment buildings lined the alleys. The usual vendors populated the streets; merchants hawked clothing, iPhones, computers, Rolex watches (of dubious origin), freshly killed animals, baked goods, and cheap liquor.

It was here, in a zero-star motel that reeked of turpentine, rotting wood and back-flow sewage, that we met with a local man named Nikkon who ran a small orphanage for girls. He was a short man with dark hair and a warm, soft voice just like his heart. Deep, vertical scars streaked his cheeks, the kind that healed long ago but never really did. I wanted to ask where they came from . . . but I didn't.

Nikkon greeted us with a big smile and introductions were passed around. His face grew darker when he told us of three little girls who were being prostituted out of a small café a few miles away. The madam had a room with a bed and the girls were being used daily by many men.

We drove across the city for our initial recon and rescue. This revealed that we could walk down a path from the main road to the slummy outdoor café and exfiltrate easily back to the road. It was busy with traffic—motorcycles, animal carts, buses, rickshaws, cars, stray dogs, and trucks zooming by, a cacophony of horns and insults, fumes of unregulated combustion wafting to the sky.

We knew we would be invisible to anyone on that road, blending in easily with the rest of the maniacs and their motorized mayhem.

Parking a short distance away, we approached the shack and saw two girls dressed in flower-covered pants and pink striped shirts standing outside the café, along with a short, fat woman in a garish dress and heavy makeup. There were a number of men inside the café all laughing and clinking glasses. Rising above the drone of traffic, we heard music playing from cheap outdoor speakers. The air was thick with stale beer and lust. Nikkon's intel told us the shack was divided by a curtain, behind which were three beds with curtains dividing each bed area. The other side of the café had a rude wooden bar that watered the patrons through grimy beer taps and dusty liquor bottles.

Yeti and Pipe Hitter donned two-way radios and earpieces as we followed G-man and Nikkon down a narrow dirt path choked with weeds and littered with plastic, rocks, and rusted bike parts. Upon closer inspection, the café was nothing more than a corrugated metal roof over a dirt floor. Several men sat outside on plastic chairs, apparently waiting their turn with the girls in the shack. They turned to look at the foreigners strolling toward them and grew visibly agitated. One, a tall, ugly man in loose-fitting clothing with fire in his eyes, jumped up and stalked off to a position about twenty yards from the café. Our eyes followed him.

Catch Dog, Yeti, and Pipe Hitter realized the security risk and moved to position themselves strategically, guarding the approach from the road, and also being ready should any of the men move in our direction. I closed on the girls with G-man and Nikkon. Another woman, perhaps fifty years old, came out of the café with a younger girl dressed the same as the first two. All three girls wore forlorn expressions of hopelessness covered by fake smiles. The madam sat them on a wooden bench, and from the hungry looks of the men, I knew they were there to be selected.

Pipe Hitter ducked his head under the low door frame and entered the café to make an assessment of the men inside. Yeti and Catch Dog remained outside. Bowing politely, I asked the madam standing outside for a picture. G-man translated. She beamed and got the girls together, oblivious to the fact that we were about to steal her human capital. I snapped the picture just for show while Samurai recorded everything with his video gear. That's when things got tight.

Yeti leaned forward and whispered that the large ugly man who stepped away was on the phone. G-man heard him say "People are here to take the girls." We had no clue who was on the other end, but—rude as it was—we weren't about to stick around to make their acquaintance. It was time to move.

Pipe Hitter stood by the door of the café. I doubted any of the men inside would have been a problem for him. They would have been downed quickly had they tried to intervene.

A nervous G-man smiled at the girls as the clueless madam spread her arms in an offering gesture. I stood beside G-man. "Tell her 'We're shutting down your business and we're taking the girls.'"

G-man translated and I watched the concern spread over the madam's face like a prairie fire. G-man then knelt and spoke softly to the girls. All three mechanically stood and followed him up the path to the road, the youngest girl in the middle holding the hands of the two older girls.

"There is no resistance in them," G-man said quietly. "They will follow a complete stranger."

"It's tragic," I said. "They are programmed to do whatever men order them to do. They no longer have a will of their own."

Although she was furious, the madam made no attempt to thwart the exodus. As often happened on rescues, timing is everything. Shock and awe are huge factors in our favor. In her mind, she knew she was wrong. That left her vulnerable to a stricken conscience. *Are they a government agency? A rival trafficker? Am I in trouble? Headed to jail?*

Our careful planning, overwhelming show of force, and swift execution left little time for her to process her overarching thought: *What just happened?*

As G-man led the girls away, he spoke gently to them, following the script we had given him.

"What are your names?"

"Devna," whispered one girl.

"Liswini. And we call her Durga," mumbled the oldest, nodding to the young girl in the middle.

"I am G-man. This is Nikkon, and this is Bruce. We are taking you to freedom. Have you ever been to school?"

Devna and Liswini shook their heads "no." Durga stared at the pathway, stepping carefully over trash and rubble, occasionally being lifted over a deep crevice by the older girls.

I walked behind them with Yeti and Catch Dog covering the exit. Pipe Hitter was to my left and Samurai orbited the scene, recording it for posterity. The older girls had slight smiles as they approached the van. Time and time again, I had to remind myself that those we rescued were still children, that despite the cruelties inflicted upon them, a spark of hope remained unextinguished. Something about G-man and the rest of us conveyed trustworthiness to these innocents. It was something about us and beyond us. There's no way we could have done this alone. During rescues, I often reflected on a scripture: *"Not by might, nor by power, but by my Spirit says the Lord. . . ."*

Once the girls were safely ensconced in the vehicle, Catch Dog and Yeti caught up to us and we all crammed into the vehicle—except for Catch Dog. It had been pre-arranged that he would give up his seat for the girls and find other transportation back to Nikkon's building. And so, he did—in his usual Catch Dog fashion.

Standing by the side of the road, he flagged down some random guy on a motorcycle, jumped on the back, shoved a few dollars into the driver's shirt and yelled, "You're taking me to this address because we're one shy of a seat." And off they went, beating us there by several minutes.

Still on high alert, watching for interference and possible pursuit, we made our way through miles of congestion. We finally arrived at Nikkon's, where a few people were waiting for us. The building housing Nikkon's orphanage was down a narrow alleyway at a dead end. The building was cement covered with peeling blue paint. There was a hand-lettered sign on the door that we later found out said "SCHOOL" in big white letters. It was attached to Nikkon's orphanage.

Entering the building, we encountered a few women who were waiting to talk to the girls. It was the first time I got a good look at their faces. They were so young. Devna told us she was twelve, Liswini was fourteen, and Durga didn't know how old she was—I guessed eight years old. *An eight-year-old being sold for sex?* They were beautiful little girls who had endured a nightmare of unimaginable horrors.

The women explained that they would soon have a new home, new clothes, good food, and a family that cared about them. Their smiles appeared briefly. This would be the start of a new life where healing would take place. It was a lot to take in, and I was thankful for Nikkon's people.

We then traveled with Nikkon to the home where the girls were to live. They were introduced to several other girls who lived there and had come out of bad situations as well. I could see the three girls relax a little as they realized this freedom might be real. They climbed on a bed with the other girls and sat cross-legged—the pose of relaxation in this Asian country. A flicker of love graced their faces. They were quiet at first, but gradually warmed, and joined in the colorful chatter.

Watching out of the corner of my eye, I saw a change in G-man as well. His apprehension was giving way to cautious acceptance. He was beginning to see the potential in what we were doing. *Ah, another soul delivered from the shackles of the slave trade.* It warmed my heart.

A Belligerent Madam

Nikkon's intel told him about a young girl held captive by a woman who prostituted her out of her home. We decided that the operation would be a quick extraction. After the day's first rescue, it was growing dark. Hopefully, this rescue would not be complicated.

Driving through the commercial area of the city with Nikkon leading us on a motorcycle, we inquired about the girl in a few shops and were told she was down a side street, just off an alleyway. *Interesting how everybody knows her.*

Nikkon insisted that we park several blocks away, along the main road, and walk to the woman's home. Yeti, thinking strategically, looked down the street, saw it was wide and clear, and asked, "Why not drive?"

Still, Nikkon—for reasons known only to him—insisted we approach on foot. This made the team nervous. Once we extracted the girl, we would have to walk one hundred yards back to the main road, exposing us to attack by others who had the good sense to drive in the first place.

This highlighted the challenge of working with untrained assets in other countries. They do not know security protocols, and it's hard to get them to understand on the fly. After a brief team conference, we accepted that we would walk to the building, extract the girl, put her on Nikkon's motorcycle because there was no room in the car, and have him drive off immediately, while we combed the street looking for any sign of trouble. By now, it was dark out, so that was to our advantage. G-man went first to scope out the home. He gave us the "good to go" signal, so we walked down the alley.

Pipe Hitter and Catch Dog entered the house, followed by myself, then Yeti and Samurai. The little girl was standing in the living room in a red dress with gold trim adorning her small frame. A stick of incense burned in a brass container. Despite the warm smell of sandalwood, it did nothing to obscure the rancid odor of cheap perfume and nicotine.

The middle-aged madam, cigarette in hand, was seated on a worn couch of scarlet cloth. Her dark clothing spoke of deep poverty. She wore heavy framed glasses that were mended at the temples, and she squinted at us as we entered. Jumping up, she greeted us in her native tongue, smiling, and opening her arms. The girl looked scared— that was understandable. A group of strange men entering the house could only mean one thing to her. Trained to show no resistance, however, she held herself still, her hands folded in her lap, her head down, her body quaking. G-man knelt and whispered to her. She nodded slightly, seemed to calm a bit, and Pipe Hitter took her hand in his, preparing to lead her away.

Realizing this was no business transaction, the woman dropped her guise as a gracious host and revealed the pit viper of hell that she really was. "No! You can't take her! She's mine!" she screamed while attempting to wedge herself between Pipe Hitter and the girl. "You pay! You pay!"

Fortunately for her, Pipe Hitter's call sign was not "Woman Hitter." Flexing muscles reserved for a 300-pound bench press, he set her firmly aside as she continued her spasmodic tirade. It was his presence, towering over her like an ivory tower of righteousness, that finally shocked her into silence. We meant business, and not the kind she wanted.

The defused madam didn't worry me too much, but the phone in her hand did. I wanted to drop her in her tracks—instead, I intoned "No, no, no!" as I ripped the phone away and crushed it. She was an evil-hearted human who forced a child into prostitution to make money for her while she watched. Unfortunately for her, loss was not on my spectrum of emotions at present. As part of our exit plan, I checked the other rooms; they were all clear. Thankfully, she'd had no time to notify her security when we walked in. *Shock and awe.*

With the perimeter secured, we were out the door and up to the main street in a flash, thankful for the cover of darkness. As with the previous rescue, the girl remained quiet and compliant, though wracked with fear. With a little coaxing from G-man and perhaps her curiosity, we got her on the back of Nikkon's motorbike. Nikkon peeled off to the hotel where we planned to meet up. With situational awareness in mind, we split up and walked to the SUV using separate routes.

Arriving at the hotel, we found Nikkon talking to the girl, whose name was Darya. She was twelve years old and had been in that home for two years. G-man told Darya she would be taken to a good home with other girls, and that she could go to school. The slightest smile creased her face, then she looked straight into my eyes as if to study me. Unflinchingly, I let her make her own assessment of who I was, what was happening, and who these people were who suddenly arrested her life with promises of a better one. I marveled at her strength.

With Darya safely in Nikkon's care, our team retired to our no-tell motel. Although we were seasoned tough guys, we were overcome with emotion at freeing these children. Catch Dog described feeling some redemption. He had seen a lot of death in combat and had taken many lives. He recognized the necessity of those actions, but it felt immeasurably better to be granting life than tearing it from the face of the earth. Tears flowed freely as my team recounted past rescues. Precious children—who had no future and no hope other than a short life span—were rescued and given new lives. We basked in the atmosphere of humility and celebration. These beautiful children were now free—to live, to grow, to choose, and hopefully someday, to return and continue the cycle of liberation.

The Slum

Our next rescue was in a village high in the mountains, once a beautiful place along the main pass but now was reduced to rubble . . . a slum, reeling from the massive loss of life after a recent earthquake. Human traffickers preyed on the multitudes of suddenly orphaned children, abducting them for local brothels or selling them abroad to be enslaved, tortured, and snuffed out of existence when they no longer amused their captors. Sadly, such predatory behavior was common after natural disasters in countries where no social safety net existed.

We endured a brief but intense drive over a serpentine mountain pass, our senses growing accustomed to high altitudes and the specter of a chance meeting with the rocks below, where introductions would be arranged by our mutual acquaintance: gravity. To our surprise, we arrived at a modern hotel. After the roach-filled motel in our first town, we did not expect twenty-first-century amenities. But G-man had gotten us good rates—I suspect he was beginning to like us—and believe me, it was nice to have hot showers.

The next morning, we met with Kasum, our local asset for this region. He was a local pastor with a burning desire to get children out of trafficking. He seemed to be a good man, and he was certainly a brave man. I felt he would also be a good influence on G-man, who was still undecided about our goals and methods. Kasum told us there were two young girls being prostituted at a local brothel.

The next day, needing intel, we ascended a narrow, winding road to the slum. The spectacular scenery in this region never failed to disappoint: high mountains and deep valleys, billowing white clouds against an azure sky, and a gentle breeze of melted snow carried by pure air. It was hard to comprehend that so much evil was happening amidst this natural beauty.

The slum was built of tin and cardboard shanties. A boulder-strewn river raged thirty feet below, the same river that flooded the village during torrential rains. Aimed at building goodwill, we spent several hours distributing rice and other supplies to the eager inhabitants of this shantytown. We met many local people and talked to the children. They were all disheveled, malnourished, and crawling with lice. The need was heartbreaking.

Driving back down the mountain to our hotel, we discussed ways to get the children out of the local brothel we had found. It was along the main road—a convenient stop for truckers and travelers to pull over, rape the girls, and vanish into anonymity. A simple plan was developed:

1. Enter the brothel.
2. Grab the girls.
3. Exit quickly.

Like I said: *simple.* When we reached the brothel the next day, however, several big trucks were parked along the road and a large, noisy, old tractor was pulling a wagon from up the road at an excruciatingly slow pace, disrupting the timing of our planned departure.

After an initial assessment by G-man and Kasum, a new plan unfolded. Yeti and Samurai would go in first, followed by myself, while the rest of the team would secure the outside of the site. We had to walk past men with hammers who were breaking boulders into rubble. Other guys worked nearby with machetes on a stand of saplings. I said a silent prayer that none of these men were regular patrons.

Arriving at the small, tin-sided brothel, Yeti and Samurai led the way. G-man and Kasum stood inside the doorway, ready to run interference with any troublesome locals. Yeti stopped by the madam and blocked her with his body, and I came up behind him. Two small girls stood at the end of a hallway washing dishes in a plastic tub of dirty water. They seemed to be around ten years old. They wore simple tops and loose-fitting pants of worn cloth. Their faces had been made up to reflect a gaiety they no longer possessed; the rouge and lipstick were smeared and ran together. The polish on their fingernails was chipped. The dark rooms to the side with the curtains drawn bothered me. They were for clients, and I didn't know if any were in use.

As I approached, the girls stopped washing but didn't look up until I whispered and motioned for them. "Come with me," I said. I knew they didn't speak English, but my intent was clear. As if they were robots, they dropped their dishrags and followed me down the hallway, past the madam—Samurai's camera in her face blocking her intervention. She was livid.

"You take my property!" she screamed in broken English.

"No . . . I'm taking these children," I said calmly as we continued to the door.

Yeti led out with Samurai videoing our exit. Now in the sunlight, I could not get over how small these girls were.

The madam pursued us to the door, and her bellicose rant gathered attention. Voices sounded from everywhere, some wanting to know what was happening, others demanding that it stop—whatever it was—until they could assess it. The workers outside the brothel stopped and stared, hammers and machetes at the ready, as we ushered the girls up the street to the waiting vehicle. Catch Dog and Pipe Hitter flanked us as we walked. We had taken the possessions of this malevolent-minded woman, and even if these laborers were not her clients, they were most likely in her employ.

With the girls safely in the vehicle, we wasted no time getting out of there. Everyone was silent as Kasum expertly raced along the gravel road back down the mountain. Aware of the shock they must be feeling, G-man spoke to our new charges.

"What are your names, girls?"

"Alina," said one girl quietly.

"Idha," said the other girl.

Alina, seated next to me, turned and stared into my soul for several minutes, invading my mind. I will never forget her dead expression. She had lost all will, she was lifeless and had nothing to shield her spirit from whatever torture these strangers had planned for her.

I looked at Pipe Hitter. He was full of rage, burning with that look we knew all too well: *Can I go back and eliminate those animals?* Catch Dog had Idha sitting beside him. He stared straight ahead, fighting the tears in his eyes. A guy tougher than nails with a heart bigger than anyone I've ever met. He often spoke of his daughters at home. That's why he could not look directly at rescued girls without an emotional avalanche. He knew what these girls must have gone through, but he had to maintain his composure to finish the rescue.

I smiled at the precious little angel who continued to bore two holes through my skull. To her I was not Bruce, I was a male, and males hurt her. G-man's voice was the only sound in the car. Like a monk at vespers after a day of silence, his voice softly assured the girls that everything was okay, that nobody was going to hurt them, that they were going to a better place. I wished we had Kasum's wife with us. Abused by men and now jammed in a car with the same, all the while being promised a spectacular life—Alina and Idha needed a mother figure right now.

We arrived at the host home where the girls would live. The family's mother, grandmother, and their girls welcomed them with love and food. The house was on the side of a hill off a basic road, a simple structure with two stories and an outhouse. The girls and the host family stood on the covered porch while we chatted with the host father. We were told that grandma would be taking care of the girls.

I studied the host family and all seemed kind and genuine. The house was neat and clean, and the porch area had several chairs and a comfortable atmosphere. The toilet was in a small building attached to the house and had a small sink. It felt like a genuinely good home for these children. The house had a great view of the valley below. As we got into our van, we could see school children in their uniforms walking up the hill on their way home from school.

Yes, this was a good place for Alina and Idha to live and heal. We left quietly and planned to return the next evening to check on them. From a nearby monastery, the final bell of the evening pealed.

Hinds Feet on High

The following morning, we made a long drive to another city to rescue more children. As with previous rescues, this one involved many hours of high altitude and winding roads, making for an arduous journey. The mountain roads were so rough that it kept all of us awake . . . except for Catch Dog. That boy could sleep through a tornado.

We finally arrived at our new location, checked in to our marginal hotel, and took the next day to rest. It was a week into this operation and we needed a break—physically and emotionally. We walked the streets, checked out vendors and hiked a few trails. I stood in the midst of the city and gazed at the far pavilions—steel gray mountains draped in white, set against an ancient sky. I thought of a line from David's psalm: *I will lift up mine eyes unto the hills, from whence cometh my help*. The magnificent peaks were a sensory overload.

We were there to extract a young brother and sister who were being prostituted out of a restaurant. According to our local asset, the boy was afflicted with a skin disease, but he was still forced to clean the restaurant and be rented out for the sick pleasures of men. This restaurant was in a rundown mall on the outskirts of the city. Driving to the location, we planned the flow of the team and their positions—who would go in, who would stay by the door, who would remain with the van. We drove around the area, getting our bearings, and parked just outside of the mall.

Yeti was first out of the van, followed by Catch Dog, Pipe Hitter, and G-man. But G-man rushed ahead of them, moving so quickly that we had to slow him down. Haste attracts unwelcome attention. Still, his enthusiasm was gratifying. When we first met G-man, he told us that rescuing children was impossible. Now he was gaining a vision for rescue and becoming a champion of the children.

Despite curbing our eager friend, we still garnered too much attention. People stopped to stare at the towering, light-skinned foreigners bulging with muscles, men who walked upright with purpose through a rundown mall like avenging angels, trying to look like your average coupon-clutching shoppers. The stores were filled with clothing, hardware, household items, and slaughtered animals hanging in the open air and crawling with flies.

Making our way through the labyrinth of connected shops, we entered the small restaurant where the children were enslaved. To the practiced eye of an operator, every detail mattered. The restaurant consisted of a main room about forty feet square, with a cooking area to the left, a small seating area to the right, and a counter separating them. Behind the counter was a small two-burner stove and refrigerator. There were some tapestries on the wall and a few posters. No sign of cameras, alarms, or other surveillance. The air smelled like tea, and something was sizzling on the stove. We counted the personnel cooking behind the counter (two), and gaged how quickly they could come around, possibly with a kitchen blade or a hammer (five seconds), or how likely they were to throw a hot pan at us (unlikely).

A lone man was in the seating area; it was probably his dinner being cooked. He was old and wrinkled and peered at us through thick glasses aiding runny eyes; he was not likely to be any trouble.

The tables and chairs were the plastic outdoor type; they would not be effective as weapons if someone tried to hurl them at us. With the main room so small, our movements would be restricted should the space fill with protesting bystanders or attackers.

Our intel told us to look for a small room to the side containing a bed. We spotted it. The door was a closed curtain; we didn't know if the room was occupied.

The team members took their assigned positions. Catch Dog sat down next to the now frightened man in the shop and tried to strike up a casual conversation. G-man and Pipe Hitter looked for the children. G-man spotted the boy in the back, mechanically sweeping the floor with his head down. His skin was mottled with seeping rashes. Near him was a little girl with a dish rag in her hands, staring up at us. Her mouth was agape, her eyes dull and lifeless, her emaciated body suddenly still. With both children in sight, it was unlikely that anybody was in the curtained room.

At the sight of the siblings, G-man lost all restraint and transformed into superman bolting from a phone booth on full afterburners. He slid the broom from the startled boy's hands and threw it against the wall; it landed with a racket. Now all heads were turned in his direction. In one practiced motion, he covered the boy's torso with a blanket and lifted him carefully into his arms. Meanwhile, Pipe Hitter walked the little girl out the door and into the sunlight, her tiny hand enveloped in his bear paw, her limbs rigid, her feet shuffling to keep up.

The madam, decked out in simple garb and plastic jewelry, stared from the back of the café but made no attempt to interfere. She was stunned. *Good! She read the script and knew her part.*

So far it had been a simple rescue, but we knew once we hit the sidewalk anything could happen. The madam had time to call her goons, and they could be close.

We quickly piled into the van and headed toward the safe house. G-man had arranged for an older woman to care for the siblings. We were concerned that the boy's skin disease would be too much for the single parent who had volunteered to care for him and the girl, but this was what we had to work with for now.

Arriving at the safe house, the team escorted the children along a long, narrow alleyway to the woman's tiny apartment. There was a separate toilet and separate kitchen somewhere down the alley. She let us in. G-man and I introduced ourselves. She looked to be in her upper forties, maybe older—it was difficult to tell, as life there was so hard that people often looked older than they were. The room was simple: a bed, a chair, and a few other things. As we looked around, I heard a commotion outside in the hallway. The little boy had taken off and was running towards the main road! Yeti ran after him and caught him a second before he would have disappeared into the busy street. Clearly, he was going to be a handful. He had a wild look in his eyes, and I wondered if the woman could handle this child.

Months later, staying in regular contact with our local assets, we learned that even though it was stressful, she did a good job raising both children. With CRI's support, she arranged multiple doctor visits to treat the boy's skin condition and deal with his hyperactivity. In time, he came to excel in school. We learned a year later that he won a dance contest in his new school. Even with the still unidentified skin disease, he was a character— the clown of the house who entertained visitors with his breakdancing.

Born into slavery, James, ninety years old is about to experience freedom for the first time in his life.

24

Binsa's Survival

A Journey Through Slavery

LIFE IS NOT EASY IN BINSA'S MOUNTAIN VILLAGE. Binsa works from sunrise to sunset. Her father also works all day. When he comes home, he is tired and disagreeable, but she knows he loves her. He sometimes plays with her and her brother. Her mother is stern; she is the one who disciplines them. She has taught Binsa many things, important things such as cooking, laundry, and other domestic chores. Binsa will need these skills when she marries and has children. Ten years old and too poor to go to school, Binsa is responsible for much of the household but still loves playing with the other children when she can.

"Binsa, we need water for dinner," says her mother.

"On my way," Binsa sings back.

She loves the walk to the narrow river that runs along her village. Icy water rushes down from the snow-capped mountains that ring the valley. The land is too rocky to dig wells, so the villagers get their water from the river. Binsa skips along, her stout legs landing securely on the rocky soil—the only home she's ever known. Swinging her empty bucket and thinking about the plump chicken her father brought home for her mother to prepare for dinner, Binsa approaches the river and notices that it is unusually high and flowing violently.

The bank is slippery, and Binsa fears falling in and being swept away like some of the other village children. She moves downstream to stand on a rock at the water's edge. She steals a few moments to look for crayfish in the shallows, but the water is rising and muddy. Finally, she scoops a bucketful of water and hurries back, water sloshing as she goes. In her haste, she brushes past a low-hanging branch and snags her purple pants. She examines the hole with tears in her eyes.

"Binsa, what's your hurry?" yells her mother as Binsa bounds through the door.

"The river is high and it scares me," she says.

"Binsa, it is normal. The river always rises after the rains. Did you get the water?"

Binsa lifts her half-full bucket.

"That is not enough, Binsa. Go fill the bucket again. And walk slowly this time."

Binsa reluctantly makes the journey again, mindful of her torn pants and wondering where to get thread to repair them. As she approaches the river, she notices that the rock she stood on is almost underwater. The river is higher. She leans carefully toward the water, dips her bucket in to fill it, and walks back. This time she does not spill the water, because she does not want to be sent back to the river.

With high mountains surrounding the valley, darkness comes early. Binsa lights the candles and the family sits to eat. The air is heavy; this is the beginning of the monsoon season. Binsa is happy to have chicken, and they all laugh as her little brother makes silly gestures, acting like a chicken as he eats. With everything cleaned up, the family lies in their beds, all in the same room. Binsa's father blows out the last candle and tells the children a short story.

Somewhere in the night, Binsa thinks she is dreaming; she wakes to the sound of screaming and feels a strange sensation of frigid water all around her. In total darkness, she is terrified as she feels herself being swept away. The water sucks the breath from her lungs. She hears cries for help all around her and finds herself holding onto a log. She is moving fast, tumbling and spinning. Water rushes over her. She coughs and spits, fighting to breathe. Heavy objects strike her legs as she is thrown into boulders and fallen trees.

She grips the floating log tightly. Finally, she hits something and stops moving. Feeling her way in darkness, she crawls onto what she thinks is solid ground and lies there heaving with deep sobs, shaking from fear and the cold that has penetrated her bones. Instinctively, she curls into a ball and fights for warmth.

As light slowly fills the valley, Binsa sees the raging river filled with wood and bodies floating by. A dead cow lies twisted and bloated thirty yards from her patch of ground. Binsa knows she has to move but has a hard time standing on stiff legs. In shock, she notices that one pant leg is torn off and the other is ripped halfway up. Her favorite purple pants—the ones she planned to mend—are ruined. Her legs and arms are cut and bruised. As the sun warms her body, pain replaces numbness. Binsa stands and cries out for a long time but no one answers, no one comes, and her tears succumb to exhaustion.

Eventually, she wanders through a devastated village, climbs a high bank, and reaches a road. She thinks she recognizes it but part of the road has washed away. She is not sure where she is or why this happened. She just wants to see her family.

Binsa crawls around the damage and wanders along the road for several hours. Coming to a group of people standing beside the road, she asks, "Can you tell me where my parents are? My village?" She names the village.

"What happened to you?" asks one of the women.

"The river took our village, and I don't know where my family is."

"That is many kilometers away, back that way," a man points out. "We are driving near there. Get in."

Binsa climbs in the car, fearful of the people but wanting to go home. After a long ride, the car pulls over. "This is the same river your village is next to. Get out here," the woman says sternly.

Binsa gets out and the car speeds away. She does not recognize the village, but maybe it's one of the ones downriver from hers. She sees many houses that are destroyed and water covering the rest. People are shouting, searching, and helping each other. They seem not to notice her.

Binsa starts walking, but she is getting farther and farther from her village. She sees devastation everywhere. Binsa knows that the waters have done this before, killing hundreds of people and destroying villages. She walks all day until a car slows beside her. Two men look her over.

She tries to get off the road but it is too narrow; steep banks descend for hundreds of meters.

"Hey, do you need a ride?" the men ask.

"No," she answers, instinctively backing away.

One of the men gets out and grabs her arm. She fights to get away, but he lifts her up and tosses her in the back seat alongside another girl around her own age. This girl lies on the seat, her hands tied behind her back, and there is terror in her eyes. In one final attempt at freedom, Binsa lashes out at her captor's eyes, but he turns his head, laughs, and ties Binsa's hands, tossing her back on the seat beside the other girl.

Neither girl speaks for the long drive. Wracked with terror, they are unloaded and shoved into a large room with other girls and boys, all shivering, some curled on the bare floor. No one looks up at the new arrivals. Binsa lies on the floor and cries. After many hours with no food or water, she is dragged to a room where she is raped repeatedly for several days until her will is broken.

Six Months Later

"Get to cleaning, Binsa," says the owner.

Binsa picks up the broom and mechanically sweeps the floor. Her head is bent, her body listless. Every movement brings pain. Her abdomen burns with hunger and abuse. Her legs are scared from the flood, and she can no longer hold her urine. Five months ago, Binsa was purchased by a woman who owns a tea shop and small restaurant. It's a small building with a few plastic tables and chairs, a narrow, dirty kitchen with a propane stove, several dingy rooms, and an open front that faces the street. Binsa must clean the floors and do dishes. She is beaten daily; any excuse will do. The owner calls her filthy names and makes her sleep on the floor in a back room. She is forced to satisfy the sick men who creep into the café, day or night. For that, there is a bed in a side room.

A few other boys and girls have come and gone. She never knows what happens to them. Today, there are two new girls in the back; they arrived a week ago. She hears them sobbing, hears their screams muffled by men with dirty hands and sour breath, hears the withering curses of the owner after the men throw down money and leave.

Binsa gets to eat once, maybe twice a day, mostly rice, sometimes a little chicken. Nothing more. She is always tired, always aches, her eyesight is blurry, her body is numb and agitated, her insides itch and seep fluid. Her thoughts stay far, far away. She tries to remember her village and the faces of her family, but they are lost in a gray mist. She no longer feels sadness; she feels nothing.

One day as Binsa sweeps, she looks out the window as a van pulls up. The doors open and some men and a woman get out, most with light skin except one man and the woman, both of whom look normal. The light-skinned men are giants, especially one in particular. Their movements are odd. They look around, and up in the air. They glance at each other, but they don't talk. Their clothing is clean, their sunglasses fancy. They move together. Two stay outside while the rest walk quickly toward the building. She hopes they are not coming for her. Her insides hurt. She glances at the owner talking with some customers in the back of the cafe. Nobody notices the strange people, nobody but Binsa. She freezes.

Some of the men and the woman enter the café with more strange looks, and then the woman comes straight toward her. Binsa clutches her broom and stares down as the woman kneels.

"What is your name?" she says in Binsa's language.

"Binsa," she says in a flat voice.

"We've come for you, Binsa," says the woman softly. "We are taking you to be free."

Binsa is rigid with fear but automatically obeys just as she has been conditioned to do. She has no will, no boundaries. No one can know the depth of her fear as she endures the daily horrors of the cafe. She shuts down and submits to sexual assault because her feelings are too strong, her shame too great, her loss of innocence beyond words. Her little girl heart is unprotected and poisoned by the evil desires of those who have lost all feelings for humanity. She is an object used to fulfill their perceived need. With her humanity stolen, her childhood erased, and her hope destroyed, she grips her broom, pushes it across the floor, and obeys the commands of the adults around her. It is all she has left . . . until the strangers arrive.

The woman gently takes her hand and leads her outside. The sun hurts her eyes. She hasn't left the café in weeks. She hears the owner's voice inside the cafe screaming hatred, the customer's outraged voices joining in, the dark tones of the strange men silencing the curses. She doesn't know if they are yelling about her or not. The woman holding her hand speaks quietly in her own language. "You are alright, Binsa. Nobody's going to hurt you as long as I'm here. We are taking you to a very good place where no men will ever touch you again. The people are kind. You will be able to play, to get new clothes, and go to school. Would you like that?"

Binsa wants to smile but she can't remember how.

As the van speeds away, Binsa stares at her new captors. Most look away. A few are crying; she is not sure why. The big one with a round head and long beard looks funny. All she can think is: *He looks like a Yeti.*

25

A Heart's Cry

ONE THING IS FOR CERTAIN—a good team is worth everything. Training together, understanding the diverse personalities, and knowing how a person will react to certain situations is critical to mission success.

Some months after our last team returned from a rescue operation, my new team arrived at the house of Minus One Eye and Zero Six in the mountains of Colorado. We were there for pre-operations training and preparation. Our team consisted of Catch Dog, Pipe Hitter, Yeti, Minus One Eye, and we were to be joined in country by Beast.

Beast was new to the team and would fly in straight from helping defeat ISIS in the Middle East. He was a medic and had worked on over 1,000 victims, treating everything from gunshot wounds to blast wounds and infections, and also performed life-saving CPR—all on the victims of ISIS. Beast was pretty hyped up when he joined us. He would need some decompression time for the built-up emotion to dissipate and for his heart to heal.

Minus One Eye had been on eleven combat tours fighting enemy combatants. He paid a big price for his courageous pursuit of a particular terrorist when he lost an eye to an enemy bullet. His teammates hunted down the terrorist, who shortly thereafter was terminated with extreme prejudice.

He and his wife spent an inordinate amount of time arranging four days of isolation training for the team. We covered technical equipment, various intelligence briefs, communications, culture, medical, and some intense physical training. This was all done at elevations at six thousand feet above sea level—quite challenging for us but fitting considering our destination. Some wonderful locals provided meals that we heartily enjoyed, along with the lively conversation. Zero Six is an amazing woman. Her expertise in running a command post is second to none. Her primary job was to stay in constant communication with our team while we were in country. She provided daily briefs, tracked our movements, and was ready if we needed emergency assistance. She was vital to our success.

The training passed quickly, and it was soon time to catch our flights and make the complicated journey to our rescue location. We were returning to the mountains of Asia—the same country as our last trip. Our goal was to create enough infrastructure to not only rescue children but to put the hurt on the bad guys, even drive them out of business. After an uneventful but grueling journey, we checked into our hotel, grabbed a little jet-lag-adjusting sleep and got right to work planning our first rescue. This was also an opportunity to fine tune the gear we brought.

"Okay, this is a test. Is everybody hooked up with cameras and radios?"

"Roger."

"Roger."

"Roger."

"Roger."

"Who's Roger?"

There's one on every team.

Local intel, received through G-man, gave us several reports of child sex trafficking in the area. Our first stop was a small teahouse off a main road where two little girls were being raped multiple times a day. From previous rescues in this country, we learned the benefits of having a local female with us when we encounter the children. While we never had problems getting the children to go with us, we wanted to minimize the trauma that those first few minutes induced in these already traumatized lives. So, as prearranged by G-man, we picked up a female volunteer whose call sign was Care.

On our initial drive by, we saw three men standing outside the teahouse talking and smoking. They had that slinky posture of men who shared a sick secret. Everything about these creatures reeked of moral corruption, from the loose way they held their cigarettes in front of their mouths as they talked, to their sloppy attire, sly smiles, and casual laughter. Clearly, they were comfortable in one another's company. *Well, time to get uncomfortable, boys.*

G-man identified the owner as one of the men. From a faint silhouette, there appeared to be at least one person inside, though it was difficult to be certain. There was a parking area next to the building. The number of motorcycles parked there corresponded to the number of men in and outside the building.

Since the sliding door of the van was on the left side, we planned to pull off to the left side of the road so the door faced the teahouse. As always, our plan involved shock and awe—as five big foreign guys calmly stormed the premises, addressed the owner, pushed back the patrons, and walked out with the trafficked children.

Of course, there were always unknowns. Would the children really be there? Would they be with a client? Who else would be there? Would they resist us? Would there be weapons? Would one of the clients be a policeman or local official? Any one of these events spelled real problems, which is why we trained as hard as we did.

Pulling up to the front of the teahouse, the van door flew open as Minus One Eye and G-man jumped out with me on their six. Catch Dog, Yeti, Pipe Hitter, and Beast fanned out behind us, securing the area around the entrance. Care followed me. I had a GoPro strapped to my chest and went straight for the panicked owner who had moved to intercept me. I pushed him aside and into the compassionate care of Minus One Eye. G-man remained outside to interpret. I entered the building with Care behind me.

The teahouse was an open room furnished with the usual: tables and not much else. *Clearly not a woman-owned business.* I saw no side rooms, nowhere for bad guys to hide, nowhere to stash children. The air was toxic with cigarettes, hashish, and something that smelled strangely like tea.

A big guy at a table—well, big for this part of the world—stood up, grabbed his motorcycle helmet and stared wistfully at the door, which we were blocking.

"Sit down," I commanded, motioning to his chair.

He sat, bewildered, and looked as if he would cry. *Okay, maybe not so big.*

As if on cue, two little girls stood up from a bench a few feet in front of me. Mindful to quell their terror, I smiled at the first girl and did not advance; she couldn't have been more than five or six years old. Her dark eyes were beautiful and mournful. I looked at the second girl and her eyes held the same, mixed with apprehension. They both wore long, pretty floral-print dresses that were frayed and dirty at the edges. Their long, sleek hair was adorned with barrettes and plastic flowers. Neither girl had shoes. They stood transfixed, holding hands and staring up at me. It was all I could do to reign in my emotions.

After one last survey of the shop and a fierce glare at Easy Rider, I stepped aside to let Care address the children.

"Hello. We are here to help you," she said, kneeling and speaking the local language. "What are your names?"

Neither girl answered, they only stared, but at least they didn't back away. Care came by her call sign honestly. I was so thankful for her. Taking the girls in hand, she led them on the long walk to freedom—roughly twenty feet— out of the prison's door and into a van and a world without abuse.

The big guy had his motorcycle helmet on by now but hadn't made much progress beyond that. *Time to make an impact, Bruce.*

"So, you like little girls?" I growled, pointing to the bench. "Is this what you like?"

Fear filled his eyes. He was shaking. As much as I wanted to put him down with my fists, I knew it'd be counterproductive. He'd just get back up . . . in a month or so . . . with medical intervention. And then where would we be?

Outside, Minus One Eye was still with the owner. I had no idea what had transpired after I handed him off, but the owner was on his knees, begging for his life. His snakeskin friends were seated on the ground with heads down. *Looks like the point was made.*

At my prompting, G-man addressed the rest of the child abusers, warning them to never do this again. I took their pictures, threatening them in a way they could appreciate: exposure. I knew this was a city of corrupt police, and we had very little backing. Still, we would return in the future to see if we could get these pseudo-men arrested.

We then exfiltrated and headed to the van. The girls were nestled in the third row with Care, who was telling them of their new freedom. There was fear in their eyes, but in time, there would be smiles as their new life materialized. They were so lovely and so young.

As we drove down the road—my adrenaline receding like an outgoing tide—I succumbed to anger and sadness, thinking of thousands of children around the world still trapped in this hell of an existence.

Catch Dog stared out the window. I knew he wanted to go back and end a few lives. His tears were flowing and he couldn't stop them. In combat, he had ended many an enemy combatant's life. He carried a heavy burden from those years. Now that he was saving lives, he was often overcome with conflicted emotions he could not express. Best to let his actions do the speaking.

Yeti often took private walks after a rescue to process everything. When he returned, it was clear he'd been crying. This was Yeti's second trip, and he would go on many more with us.

I felt blessed to work with these heroes. They were the best of the best, men of character and vision. And when it comes to a team, it's all about character—that elusive quality that expresses its substance in integrity, honesty, uprightness, and honor. Gifts and talents may be abundant, but without character they are dangerous offerings.

I did not want people who were interested in racking up the rescue count. I only wanted men and women who put the victims first and were willing to do whatever it takes to free them. This required discipline—to not act as we wanted to in the moment but to appreciate the results of our actions. Villages have been burned down simply because someone misjudged the situation. I have worked with many people who were gifted, but character was the vital quality that made them effective.

These thoughts flowed as we made the drive to the safe-house. The two little girls—still silent—walked toward the house hand in hand with Care. They looked so frail. All eyes were on them as they stepped into a new day of liberation.

The home was quite nice. We were greeted by the hosts and met a little girl G-man had rescued a few weeks prior to our arrival. She was painfully thin, with short brown hair, and new clothes that draped her bones. She offered a smile but made no eye contact, though she did light up when she saw the new girls come in.

This triggered emotions for all of us. My self-control in tatters, I walked outside and broke down. Yeti disappeared on his walk. Catch Dog and Minus One Eye vanished. Beast disappeared as well. The malevolence of human behavior and the depths of depravity are incomprehensible to the moral mind.

We stayed outside until the children settled in. With our composure partially intact, we took turns giving gift bags to the children: personal products, a jacket, and some food. This was an extremely important part of our operations. We take care of the children we rescue. Our Survivor Care program supports each rescued child monthly and provides a follow-up to check on their care. (More on this in Part IV.)

An Unplanned Detour

Later in the day, through one of G-man's assets, we heard about a family that was in labor slavery. G-man wanted to rescue them, but we did not have the funds. The initial rescues were not the main expense; it was the aftercare that required the most support. Still, we took the long drive to visit this family, see their conditions, and hear their story.

Arriving at the brick kiln, we drove down a long gravel road and discovered a number of people toiling in the cool mountain air. G-man told the driver to turn around and face outward towards the main road so we could exit quickly if needed. Fortunately, we were never accosted by the owner or his goons. If they were there, they remained phantoms.

We found the family laboring at the brick molds—two parents, two girls, and a young boy. They struggled at various tasks, moving lethargically, and looking hopeless. It was painful to watch—in our western clothes, bellies full from lunch, tickets for our departure safely stowed as ones and zeros on some server—while these innocent souls faced a lifetime of servitude that they could not endure nor comprehend.

Upon our arrival, the father looked up, leaned on his shovel, smiled wearily, and extended a bony hand. Through stained teeth and acrid breath, he spoke of their enslavement, the chronic sickness of his wife and children, and how they could never get ahead of the debt they owed. His rail-thin wife looked on, pleading silently to whatever gods had sent us, her heart screaming silently in a language no man could ignore. *Free us!* Our hearts were wrenched. G-man offered food and water and promised to return. We were careful to not hold out hope for a rescue we could not provide.

As we returned to the van, the discouragement of the team was palatable. We had no funds to get this family set up with a new life: housing, medical, school, and monthly support. Also, our time was short; we were returning home in a few days. Yet this family really captured the heart of Catch Dog. He was adamant that we needed to rescue them . . . but how?

This family became known as The Brickfield Five.

One hundred forty-four rescued children receive a hot meal at a rescue center. Most of the children only ate three to four times per week prior to this picture.

26

The Brickfield Five

By Catch Dog

If a man would stop trying to focus on making people think he's a good man and just focus on being a good man, the world will see him for what he is.

Catch Dog's Grandpa

I'D ONLY BEEN ON A FEW MISSIONS. Up to that point, I was still an inexperienced operator. By no means did I have the tactical knowledge or leadership that the Professor had. I always saw myself as a grunt: drop the tailgate, load me up, tell me when to jump out. I'm the Professor's *yes* man. If he wants it, he gets it.

Anyway, we went in and we saw this family at a brick kiln during our pre-op investigation for a future rescue, and at first, we saw the man and woman. And it kinda bothered me, the fact that we saw two people that were in debt bondage slavery. But then I glanced around and saw the three little ones that was following behind them. And one of them—the baby—was around two, no older than three, for sure. And I mean, that baby was covered in mud. From her feet to her shoulders, all the way back. You could tell that those owners had the little ones walking in mud all day long. And the folks had that hopeless look in their faces, just lost, lifeless.

So, me being me, or any normal person on the team, I said, "Oh my God. We've gotta get these people outta here. We've gotta get them out now, Professor!"

So Professor, he says, "Look, we're running out of funds. We don't really have the money to pull them out right now. Because what good is it gonna do to pull the family out if you can't set 'em up with a job or a business or housing or whatever. And then they're gonna get picked right back up by the slave owners, or murdered or sold or beat or whatever."

And again, due to my lack of leadership experience at that time, I had a really hard time dealing with the tough decisions we have to sometimes make. Sometimes you have to make that hard decision. It's just really sad. And I know that it was a really tough decision for the Professor because the weight always comes down on leadership.

If leadership has to make that tough call, everybody's like, "Man, that's a tough call." But at the end of the day, we're not the ones that had to make it. We don't have to live on that decision, good, bad or indifferent. Because of the experience of the Professor on this trip, he knew about the overall safety and well-being of this family. If we just snatched them out and stuck 'em somewhere on the side of the road or tried to put 'em somewhere, they would absolutely be chopped up. They'd be killed, their children would be raped, they'd be sold, they'd be punished for trying to escape. And so there again, through his leadership, Professor knew that it was a hard decision to leave 'em where they were, but that's a little better situation than them gettin' caught just a few days later because they didn't have anywhere safe to go.

Well, my emotions got really pulled at that moment—one hundred percent just raw emotion saying: *Here's a couple kids: let's grab 'em, let's go, let's get 'em. Anything happens, we take care of the threat. As long as we get those babies out or get that family out, get 'em to sanctuary, nothing else matters.*

Now, I won't ever forget it—we drove back to our staging area where we was gonna turn in for the night. We all ordered food and I was sitting across the table from Yeti. Minus One Eye was beside me and Professor, he was across the table on Yeti's side. I always order chicken chow-mein and a Mountain Dew. G-man always makes fun of me for that. He says, "Catch Dog always orders the same thing: chicken chow mein an' Mountain Dew."

He always laughs at me. He likes to say, "Catchy sounds like a cowboy when he talks."

And I say, "Yeah, I reckon I do."

But I was sitting there and I had just got my food and I was picking at it. I couldn't eat. I was sick. I was upset and just thinking how I'm sitting there with this plate of food instead of rescuing this family, and all because of money, just because we don't have the funds.

It's not that we don't have the skillset or have enough people on this team to perform this extraction. That's not the case. The only reason this family is not gonna be saved, and they're gonna remain slaves for the rest of their lives, is because we don't have the money to give them a place to live, set them up with a business, whether it's a fruit stand or a tea shop or a coffee shop—something where they can sustain life after we leave.

And I just couldn't wrap my brain around the fact that I would go home in three days, and I would look my family in the eyes, and. And my small kids, they'd go like they always ask me: "Oh Daddy! Did you rescue all the kids?"

And I knew that question was gonna come up whenever I got home. And I just couldn't...I couldn't go home and look at my kids and say, "Yeah, yeah baby, we rescued all of 'em." All the while knowing deep down inside my heart that we had to leave an entire family behind.

It was one of those things where it was like: *Man, I wish that we wouldn't even have seen 'em. I wish that we never even would have went out there and looked at 'em.* I'm sure that sounds like an excuse or the easy way to do things, but it's like: *Well, if I don't see the problem, then I don't know there's a problem.*

That makes it easier to deal with than: *Oh yeah, by the way, I put my eyes on that family of five. I walked into where their man-made hell that they call life is, and I just left 'em there because we didn't have just a couple thousand dollars extra.*

And I know it don't seem like a lot, but we'd already spent tens of thousands of dollars during this trip on other people that were accounted for, and other children that we rescued, and everything that goes into getting them relocated. So, we were just strapped. We didn't have anything left.

So, I'm sitting there picking at my food. I look at Professor. Minus One Eye was there, Yeti was there. And I was like: "Professor, there's gotta be something we can do. There's no way we can just leave these people here and it would be okay."

Then Professor come up with this idea. "Well, I'll tell you what, Catchy. You find a way to make a few grand tonight, and in the morning, we'll go get 'em. We'll go pick 'em up. We'll set 'em up with a spot. We'll give 'em a business, and everything will be good to go. But outside of that, unless God provides a way for this to happen, it's not gonna happen."

And there again, me being me and being emotional-minded…to be honest with you, a little selfish—a lot of operators, they won't admit that—I absolutely felt selfish for the fact that I didn't want to go home without all the good feelings, all the warm-and-fuzzies: *Hey man, we did a great job!*

But the Professor was looking at it from a crew leadership standpoint. He's like: "I wanna rescue these kids just as bad as anybody else does, but it's not gonna help this family to pull them out and then they get picked up three or four days later because we didn't set them up with the means to be able to take care of themselves."

So I kinda got upset; I got a little emotional. I looked down and said, "Well, alright then, Professor. I've gotta try something. We've gotta do something."

And that's all I knew. I didn't have a clue where to start, what to do, who to talk to. I just prayed. I was like: "God, look. I know you sent us here. And God, I know you protect us, you lead us, guide us, and direct us, and we need a miracle. Now! We absolutely need a miracle right now."

And God knew my heart. It's not one of those prayers: "Oh, I'm tough and I ain't going home if I don't save 'em." It didn't have anything to do with that kind of crap. It's just…I couldn't. I couldn't look my family in the face at that point, knowing what we had to leave behind.

So I went upstairs to the room. I got my phone out. I looked at Yeti and said, "Hey bro. I need you to help video this."

And he's like: "What are you doing?"

I said, "Man, I've got nothing to lose at this point. Our people already know we're somewhere in the world, and they know we're rescuing kids. That's what we do. So I'm just gonna straight-up come out and ask 'em. I'm gonna explain the situation and ask 'em and say, 'Look, if you can come up with the money, help us come up with the money so we can rescue this family.' And if not, I'll stay back until we can figure out how we're gonna raise the money, and then we'll go in and pull 'em out and we'll fly home. There's gotta be something we can do."

So Yeti's like: "Alright man, I'm in."

So he done the video, a little two-minute video, that's all it was. I said, "We found a family. It's a husband, wife, and three kids. And we don't have the funds to pull 'em out. Look, we're not leavin' 'em. I don't know how we're gonna take care of 'em or how we're gonna protect 'em. I don't know if we're gonna have to go in and rescue 'em and all of us hang out for a week or two 'til we figure some-thing out, but we can't come home without 'em."

And I just left it up to God and the goodness of people that believe in us, believe in the mission, and believe in the good that CRI does—that it's not some kind of scam or gimmick.

I told 'em in the video, I said, "Look, I've got ten hours. We have ten hours to make this decision or this family's not gonna get rescued."

And then we hit the submit button, man, and we uploaded it to Facebook.

Minus One Eye came down after we put up the video. Now, he has a larger background in leadership than what I have because of his military background and things, and he looked me and said, "You really put Professor in a bad spot."

Now, Minus One Eye is the dog that everybody looks up to. It's like: "That guy's just cold, or hard or mean or whatever." But it's not really that. He's strictly business. It's by-the-book, and this is the standard, and this is what the standard's gotta be.

So, in his mind, I broke the standard because I had raised the question: "Is there something we can do? Is there some way to change the situation? Can't we just go get 'em?" It was my "We're not leaving 'em" attitude.

One Eye, he came down on me. He's like: "You got Professor in a bad spot because you challenged this thing, and now you're like: 'Hey, we're goin' and we're not leavin' and we're doin' this.' Where do you think that puts the Professor?"

I could see it now. Professor already had everything lined out based on what we had with money and funds for, and now I've put additional stress on him. He's probably thinking: *Well, now I've got this operator that's gonna go off, do this own thing, and not listen or whatever.* So, it just made things really bad.

One Eye showed me how I put things in a bad spot because now instead of focusing on the last mission that we had planned—the insertion points and extraction points and meeting up with the local contacts to make sure the mission we had already planned for that last day was a go—now I've thrown a monkey wrench in things and it was really unneeded stress. Fact is, you gotta make the hard decision sometimes. We hate it but that's part of being a leader.

So, there I was thinking I'm doing something good because "we're diggin' in our heels in right here; we're gonna save this family." And then it's brought to my attention by One Eye that "You really slowed things down for the rest of the process, man."

Well, I looked at him and I'm like: "Man, I'm sorry, Dude. I apologize. I didn't see it like that because I wasn't looking at it through that top-tier leadership perspective. I was just looking at it from a team member's perspective, just a guy with a big heart that don't wanna leave anybody. I don't wanna lose anybody. I wanna help everybody."

But it don't always work like that in the real world. You learn those things as you grow as an operator and as you get more leadership opportunities.

So me and Yeti, we sat up all night long, and I mean literally all night, 'cause we couldn't see what was coming in on the PayPal. And I'm sitting there looking at Yeti, and I was like: "Man, I don't know what we're gonna do. This has gotta work. 'Cause if it don't, not only am I not gonna be able to rescue this family, but now I'm marked as that guy that don't listen or go against the grain when he gets his own little idea in his head."

So Yeti calmed me down. He's down. He don't care. He's like: "Man, we got this. I'm in. Let's go."

Well, now we're on this goose chase for the next ten hours. I was really doubting myself as an operator as well, because I had so many emotions going off at once.

The next morning, I'm in the hallway with Yeti sitting right outside Professor's room. And the door flies open. Minus One Eye comes out and he has this look on his face. I'm just sitting there staring up like a kid waiting on Christmas. He looks at me and smiles and says, "Well, Catchy... God showed up."

Me and Yeti looked at each other. "What?"

Then he said, "God showed up, Catchy. We're going to get 'em." And he walked down the hall, cool as can be, going to get a cup of coffee.

Man, I was overran with emotions. I cried. I was all upset. Professor comes out, and I was like: "Man, are you serious?"

Turns out we had actually taken in three times the amount that we had asked for. It was just unbelievable. We're pumped. We're excited. We're hugging each other. We're thanking God. We're praying. We're like: "God, you showed up. God, this was not me. This was not any individual. God, this was you. You set aside this time for us and you made a way where there was no way, and you did it through people we didn't even know!"

So, we was able to greenlight the exercise. We rolled in...and I won't never forget it, man. We got there, we slipped in the backside of that brickfield. We got the mom, the dad, the two older kids and the little baby—that two-year-old, covered in mud—you don't ever forget that. I looked that baby in the eyes, and his mom and them, they were moving fast. And I looked at that baby and said, "Come on, then." And she just walked up to me and had her arms up. She's like: "I don't know who you are, I don't know where we're going, but I trust you."

She just didn't care. She never seen a white dude in her life, let alone a white dude with a beard, a ball cap a radio and all this operator stuff. That baby, she's like: "I'm so miserable where I'm at, I'm literally willing to go with anybody to get me outta here." That baby saw something in us that was real.

So I reached down and picked her up, and the boys got the rest of the family out, and I walked out with that baby on my hip, just like if it had been my kid, my two-year-old. It was no problem whatsoever. We got in the car, and everybody was just pumped and excited and high-fiving each other. And the mom's laughing and the dad's laughing. Then you got the baby looking at Minus One Eye, looking at his tattoos, laughing and pointing. Hadn't never seen tattoos, I guess. And it was probably one of the best days of my life. It was a time you won't never forget. You won't never. You won't never forget that.

I guess that's what I love most about CRI. It's not a one-man show. It's a team. And more than that, we're family. Because no matter what—right, wrong, or indifferent— we're family. And like any other family, I may argue with Professor, or Professor may argue with me, or we may all of us get on each other at some point, but when it's time to roll, we'll fight the devil himself to the very end to protect each other. You can't get that anywhere else.

In CRI, you have a group of men and women that are willing to come together and work for free because it's the right thing to do. We don't get paid. We don't get big medals. The news stations don't come and write stories on us. People don't knock on my door and say, "Hey man, you did a good job." You just go unnoticed and unrecognized, but at the end of the day, none of us want the recognition. All we want is be able to go back and rescue more families and kids.

My grandpa used to say, "If a man would stop trying to focus on making people think he's a good man and just focus on being a good man, then the world will see him for what he is."

And that's all I ever wanted. Days like this will always remind me that there was a time in my life when I was a good man.

The feet of children waiting to wash off the mud.

27

Minus One Eye's Perspective

By Minus One Eye

I FIRST HEARD OF CHILDREN'S RESCUE INITIATIVE through a co-worker who was getting ready to go on a rescue mission. The cause immediately resonated with me, and I followed in earnest as he shared bits and pieces of his experiences through social media.

But as it often does, life got in the way and I was quickly wrapped up in the day-to-day activities that occupy us all. Then, scrolling my news feed one morning, I saw the video testimonials from all the team members at the conclusion of their last rescue mission. Each interview struck me like a bolt of lightning, one jolt after another. The last interview I watched included the sentence, "I came here to rescue children, but what ended up happening was these kids rescued me." This final lightning bolt actually pushed me back into my chair.

For the longest time, I have struggled to cope with the emotional aftermath of twenty-six years in the military, including multiple combat tours. I couldn't define it then, but subconsciously I knew my soul needed healing. The cause of these men struck me as anointed. The impact they had was literally life changing to those they rescued. The impact to themselves, obviously transformative. My spirit longed for the feelings they were expressing in these interviews. I knew in that moment I had to join, and I hoped they would accept me.

Several months later, I found myself in pre-mission training with the same men I had seen in those interviews. Needless to say, I was a little anxious. My whole military career had been about tactics, aggression, and overwhelming force in one form or another. As the new guy to the team, I watched these "gentle giants" prepare to enter areas just as dangerous as I had ever been, only without the equipment and support that was critical to mission success during my military days. It struck me that this was a new kind of courage that I was witnessing. I tried to assimilate quickly and add value where I could, but I also did a lot of listening and observing.

What I discovered was that these were, first and foremost, men of God. Warriors, yes, but Christians first. And they walked the walk of this title in an unassuming, yet confident manner. Unlike the team room banter I was accustomed to, these men spoke of family, principles, scripture, purpose, and salvation. These men included prayer and faith in their tactical plans. They never pressured me to believe as they did, but they also did not let me shrink away from the discussion due to my discomfort or background. I came out of that pre-mission training with a new purpose: to approach this mission with an "empty cup," and to be receptive to whatever experiences may come my way. As we parted ways after the pre-mission training I sat at length in solitude, contemplating the things I had just witnessed and wondering what place this entire experience would have in my life.

The night before I left on the mission, I had the first open conversation with God that I can remember since I was a child. Naively, I made a "deal" with The Man Upstairs that I would be open to any messages He may want to send me, but in exchange, he would grant me the relief and healing (I think I may have actually used the word "redemption.") that my soul was in such desperate need of. Heck, if rescuing young children from the depths of evil couldn't balance the books for the mistakes I made in my life, what could, right?

My first few rescues with the team were over too fast for me to truly take in the magnitude of what we were doing. I had a job to do, a sector to secure, a strategic mission to accomplish. I definitely was just trying not to let the team down and to make sure the kids got out safe. All that changed about mid-trip, when we were confronted by our first defiant proprietors of a brothel where the kids were especially abused, damaged, and traumatized. As we were pulling the kids out, the smirk on the owner's face made something inside me snap. Although I didn't speak his language, his meaning was crystal clear: "I'll have another five kids here tomorrow to replace the ones you're taking." The deepest, darkest parts of my character and emotions—the ones I thought I had buried long after leaving combat—came rushing full force to the surface as if they had never gone away. I was consumed with a rage that needed an outlet. It was only the quick thinking of a fellow teammate who noticed the change come over me and stepped between me and my target that deterred me from my objective. "Not in front of the kids," he whispered in my ear.

Shaking, I evacuated with my team and those precious children into the van, and we left the area. My seat was right by the children. In previous missions, once we got back into the van we would try to calm and ease the children by smiling, waving, being silly, etc. Most of the kids were understandably terrified and confused. Most eventually relaxed when the aftercare workers would explain that they had been rescued and were going to a safe, healthy place where they could start school, play, eat, not be abused any longer, etc. I tried to swallow all the darkness down and do the same. Only this time was different. The eyes of these children told the story of extreme psychological abuse. The horrors they endured at the hands of some of the vilest creatures to ever inhabit the earth was evident on open wound marks from beatings and the hopelessness in their countenance. Every time the van would hit a pothole on the dusty road, one of the kids—a five-year-old boy— would wince in pain from the beatings he had endured. No consoling, no smile, no funny face, no words of encouragement could break through to them. Their innocence had been stolen, their spirits broken, and I did not have the tools to fix it.

This only added fuel to my rage and fed the darkest demons of my soul. It was all I could do to keep my composure and look away from the children, lest they see an all-to-familiar evil in the eyes of one of their would-be rescuers. As soon as we were able to drop them off at their caregivers' facility and ensure their safety, I quickly left to try to get control of the tidal wave of darkness that was consuming me. Without an object to vent on, the emotions poured out of me in cascades of tears and sobs.

Later that evening, I spoke with Bruce about my experience. Instead of the restoration I was searching for, my spirit was being drawn and quartered with diametrically opposing emotional extremes. How could I be doing something so good as rescuing innocent children from literal hell, yet simultaneously be consumed with the absolute darkest of human emotions that also define hell? Despite his best efforts to ease my burden, I felt lost, confused, and . . . dark.

As of writing this, it has now been several days and several rescue missions since that low point. I have had a lot of time to meditate on this and (thankfully) have been able to process a lot of these conflicting emotions with my fellow teammates. I still don't have all the answers. If I let myself go there, I can concentrate on the evil perpetrators and their actions that make CRI a necessity, and quickly get consumed by the darkness that wells up from deep within. But I have also learned some truths that I choose to concentrate on instead:

- No greater light exists in this world than the smile and eyes of a child who regains an ounce of their innocence, even within the first few minutes of freedom.

- I was naive to think that this rescue mission had anything to do with me "finding redemption." It has nothing to do with me at all. It has everything to do with the kids, and they are the ONLY thing that it's about.

- I will never allow my own needs or emotions to contribute to damaging whatever shred of innocence may be left in a child we are rescuing.

- Evil does exist. True, unadulterated evil that does things that even nightmares can't fathom. But good also exists. It exists in the brave men that I served alongside on that mission. It exists in the network of caretakers who will be selflessly caring for these rescued children long after we have left. It exists in the eyes and smile of a child playing freely for the first time in their life. It exists in the innocence of these children who will eventually be healed and form a generation of survivors who will also spread good in the world. And where good and light exist, evil and darkness must retreat.

I wish I could conclude my insert by telling you that I left that mission with the same sentiments shared by those who started me on this journey. It's honestly still too raw and real for me to definitively say. But I can tell you that I am changed. I will never look at a storefront the same way again. I can't stand the sight of bricks. And I know that I have a lot of emotions to sort out. I feel a draw from my spirit that I need to figure out and understand. I can tell you that the conversation level between me and my God has—and will continue to—increase as I try to process all of this. I can definitively say I will not be able to truly relax or peacefully rest while I know what is happening to a young boy or girl somewhere in the world right this very second. I will continue to support CRI in some form or another, likely until I leave this life. After all, the children are calling.

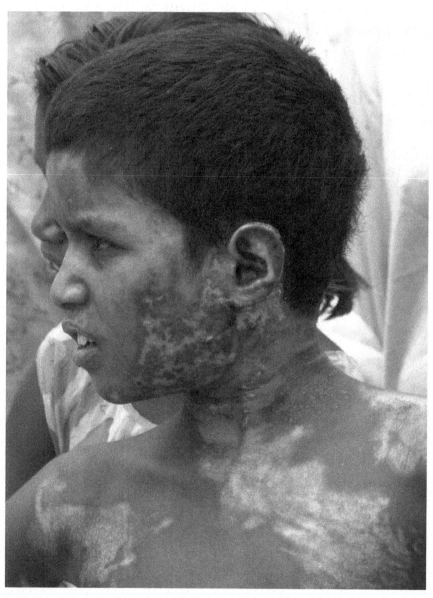

This slave boy had acid thrown on him to punish his father for being sick and not working.

28

Yeti's Story

By Yeti

As I BEGIN THIS CHAPTER, I realize that the occurrences which led me to be a part of and grow so integrally involved with Children's Rescue Initiative were nothing short of divine connection.

My introduction to human trafficking began in January of 2010. I was part of a security detail during the aftermath of the Haitian earthquake. We were assigned to protect a compound and help find additional survivors of the earthquake, people who could be brought to the facility for help. In our day-to-day travels, I began to notice young boys and girls who were dressed up and working as "housemaids." At the time, it looked peculiar, but as our time in-country grew longer, it looked normal, business as usual, part of their customs.

Inquiring from the locals, I discovered that the "housemaids" were children in forced labor for a debt owed by their parents. They called these children "restaveks," and this was indeed human trafficking and forced labor, right out in the open with no one doing anything about it. Sadly,

I didn't do anything about it either, and as soon as the security detail was over, off we went back to our cushy western world. But the seed of what I had seen (and ignored) was planted.

Fast forward a year. I hosted a security training in my hometown where several practitioners from around the world were in attendance. One such student was Bruce Ladebu, the owner and founder of Children's Rescue Initiative. He and I hit it off, and a friendship was created. I began following him and his cause on social media, but I found myself wanting to do more. I felt drawn, compelled to serve this cause. And so, I stepped up and began spending more time, money, and my own resources to make it happen.

It wasn't until the fall of 2015 that I could actually commit to assisting on a rescue. The thought of going on a rescue was gnawing at my soul for quite some time, but a business contract kept me from participating until then.

As I prepared for my first rescue operation with CRI, so many emotions flowed within me—anticipation, sorrow, anger, and rage. We spent the prior months training and learning about the objective. Our in-country contact was new to CRI, as it was our first mission into this part of Southwest Asia. This was going to be primarily a reconnaissance mission to determine where and how we would conduct rescues in this country in future missions. It turned out to be a life-changing experience for me.

From day one in that mountainous Asian country, we knew we would be rescuing children on this trip. Our team was poised and ready. G-man, our new in-country contact, was a little hesitant at first, but once he realized what he was capable of, that hesitation turned into a fire that lit the whole country aflame.

I'll never forget one of my very first rescues. The images, sights, sounds, and details are burned into my memory forever. This is what I've been called to do. This is my purpose.

The location was a tea/coffee shop on the side of the road. It was a frequent watering hole for delivery and construction drivers, a relatively small place. No one who happened to drive by would see that it possessed a very real hell to three young girls—girls as young *and younger* than my own daughters. Just beyond the main serving area for patrons was a small, dark, musty room. In the far end of that room was a tattered and stained mattress.

After getting our briefing by G-man, we headed out to the shop. I won't go into the logistics that we do regarding planning, advance work, and surveillance; that's not relevant to the flow of my story.

Geared up and ready, we pulled up to our rescue site. Our team exited the vehicle with intent and focus. Although we stood out as foreigners, we were greeted by the owner with smiles and accolades. "How bizarre," I thought—until the reality of her actions kicked in. She was under the assumption that we were there as solicitors for her side business. The anger, rage, and disgust began to boil up within. I could read it on my teammates' faces also. But we had to hide this for the moment. G-man spoke the native language to the owner and informed her that we were there for the girls.

Her face forever burns in my mind—the smile of disgusting pride she showed as she went into that dark back room and returned with those three precious babies for our inspection. *Is this how this works? These children are put on display like some type of buffet option?*

The shame, fear, and trembling these young girls displayed as a group of westerners "inspected" them and determined their worth sickened me. They were trained, broken, and soulless. The owner beamed; she expected a very good business day indeed.

Our team was poised and ready. Our zones were covered with security. The atmosphere shifted. Patrons sipping their tea and coffee looked up, sensing something odd. The bookkeeper grew nervous. Others around the establishment took notice as G-man spoke again to the owner,

"No, no, no. We are *taking* these girls *with* us. What you are doing is vile and deplorable."

Her expression went from absolute joy to horror! She knew what we were then—not patrons, but liberators. And there was nothing she, her patrons, or anyone else could do to stop us. With the efficiency of training, we escorted the girls away as G-man explained to them why we were there—that they were no longer property, but free.

Finally in the vehicle with our precious cargo, G-man did his best to ease their tormented minds. I could barely look at them. Their faces were empty and blank. They had removed themselves from life to endure the horrors and torturous lives they endured. The reality of what was happening to them hadn't even remotely begun to sink in. They had heard every story and lie before. In their minds, they were just being taken to a new place of hell. But unbeknownst to them, this was the first day of their new lives, their first day of freedom.

Many months later we returned to the area and visited the safehouse where they were residing. The blank and empty stares were now filled with happiness and joy. They were being educated, fed well, and taken care of like any child deserves—with love, respect, and honor. I wept to see the transition. These actions are what sealed it for me. I am, and will always be, a defender of the defenseless. I could go on and on about the impact of what we are doing, but I will leave it at this: CRI is where I was divinely connected to intricately be a part of defending the defenseless. It's woven into the very fabric of who I am. I thank the Professor for being the visionary to plant, water, and bring this seed into full fruition.

From the moment I left the safety of my home to venture out and help these brave men and women bring liberation to those we rescue; I knew I had to continue. The rescues persisted, and I have been able to go on several more. Each one was emotionally charged and as liberating to myself as to those we rescued.

We have expanded CRI from that first mission, because so much more goes into this organization than just rescues. That is only the tip of the spear. We host rescue training, medical training, aftercare training, logistical training, and advanced and specialized courses. We have turned CRI into a well-rounded, beneficial process that does everything Bruce has hoped for—to restore and raise up those we rescue as well as those of us working to bring them to freedom. We are developing partnerships with other organizations, working in tandem both overseas and stateside. We at CRI have all come to one agreement:

If not us, then who?

If not now, then when?

We can ALL do something. As our teams continue to go out into harm's way to rescue those who need it most, we feel confident that what we are doing is making a positive impact on those we've rescued.

There isn't a day that goes by that I don't think of the children still trapped in a life of violence and abuse. I cling to Psalm 82:3-4, and know that I am doing all I can, for my actions speak louder than any voice could.

Defend the weak and the fatherless;
uphold the cause of the poor and the oppressed.
Rescue the weak and the needy;
deliver them from the hand of the wicked.

29

Quiet Reflections

Thanks

The van rolls along and the team is quiet. I look back at each of these brave warriors.

Catch Dog gazes out the window. He can't look at the girls we just rescued. In times past, when he looked into their lifeless eyes, he could not contain his emotion. His eyes leaked buckets.

Minus One Eye glances at Catch Dog. His eye is moist, and I can tell he is having a hard time containing a combination of anger and joy. He is like a coiled spring ready to mete out justice. He could do it, too. As a highly trained and decorated combat veteran, he has the skills. Fortunately, he also has the discretion.

Yeti, constantly aware of his surroundings, has drifted off to someplace far away, maybe imagining the wonderful future these children would now have. He is as tough as they come.

Pipe Hitter is in the same state. Maybe he is imagining a better life for the children, or maybe something far more sinister, such as dealing with the bad guys. He has terminated lots of bad guys in the past; it isn't hard to see where his thoughts could go.

Catch Dog glances over at me. Our brief exchange says everything. From another life in combat, he is now seeing the other side of justice. Saving the lives of child slaves is a whole new paradigm.

Beast is one tough Marine. He is quiet, processing it all.

G-man, a true hero, sits with three precious girls in the middle seat. Surrounded by the best security on the planet, they are safe and will be well cared for.

Warriors willing to travel to the far ends of the world to rescue children: I salute you.

The Professor

PART IV

Where Are We Today?

30

Afiya's Escape

From the International Market

AFIYA AWOKE TO DARKNESS. *Where am I?* The smell of diesel fuel, salt water, grease, and muck sloshing in the bilges below . . . it slowly came to her addled mind: *I'm on a boat . . . but why?* Now seasick, she threw up, crying between heaves, her empty stomach forcing up nothing but bile. As clarity returned, she heard other children crying and retching, but she could not see them. Cold steel bars met her reaching hands. *I'm in a cage! How long have I been unconscious?* A blanket was bunched under her. She curled in a ball and wept uncontrollably. The nightmare continued. Hunger gnawed at her stomach, and her bladder was nearly bursting. "Somebody . . . help me," she groaned.

Afiya was a sad child growing up in a poor area of an African city. She and her family often worked together smashing rocks to make gravel, selling it for pennies. Her mother washed other people's clothes, and her father labored long hours at construction sites and suffered many injuries. Most nights he limped home and collapsed, needing cheap liquor to fall asleep.

When Afiya turned thirteen, her mother told her she must find a job that paid more than making gravel. Their village was on the edge of the nation's capital, surely, she could find opportunities there. So, her mother dressed Afiya in a long flowered dress, a white shirt, and sandals, braided her hair and put her on a bus to the city center. It took several hours through heavy traffic. It was an overwhelming experience for her; she rarely traveled beyond her village.

She found the building she was looking for. The sign said "Government Job Agency." It was a single-story building with posters in the windows listing the countries you could work in and the jobs you could do.

At the sight of the posters, Afiya was paralyzed. She wanted to bolt. She did not know much about her government or the business world or that her country was run by a ruthless dictator. She only knew unending poverty and her father's anguish each morning as he crawled off the floor and headed to work.

With fear gripping her heart, Afiya walked into the building, gazed at the clean, spacious lobby, and approached the first person she saw.

"I am here to get a job, please?" she stammered.

"Go to the desk over there," said a tall, haughty woman in a business suit. "Give them your name and wait your turn like the others."

Afiya's name was finally called, and she was led into an office where she sat before an older man behind a desk. His face was hard, his skin glazed. Afiya shuddered, feeling his gaze slide up and down her body. His mouth smiled, but his cold, dead eyes remained fixed. Afiya knew she didn't belong here.

"Why are you here?" he asked, his words smooth and terrifying.

"Please sir . . . a job?" asked Afiya.

"What do you do?"

"I help my mother do laundry. My family makes gravel. I can read a little. I can cook or sew."

"How old are you?"

"Thirteen, sir."

"Hmmm . . . " he said, appraising her. "Stand up. Now, turn around . . . slowly. Do it again. Let me see all of you."

Afiya stumbled in a circle, her long limbs quivering, dizziness nearly knocking her over, a deep foreboding forming in her soul. She had never been to a job interview before. Certainly, this was not what she expected. Instinctively, she wanted to flee, rush home, scream that it was all a mistake, that something had gone terribly wrong, but her mother's voice rang in her head: *You must come home with a job. Your father can't work much longer.*

"Are you willing to travel for work?" asked the man, his eyebrows holding the question in the air.

"How far? Where will I go?" she asked, biting her lower lip.

"It doesn't matter! If you want to work, you must go where we tell you, or you cannot make any money."

"I need to ask my mom if it is okay."

"Where is your mom?" he asked with a smirk.

"In our village, outside of town." She told him the name.

"Oh, that is two hours to travel there," he said gravely.

"Yes, by bus," she whispered, head lowered.

"Listen to me," said the man, leaning toward her. "If you want this job—if you want to help your family—you need to leave today. We can send a message to your mom letting her know you got the job. I'll have one of my staff give you the details. But this opening won't last."

"Well . . . I guess I could—"

"Here, sign this paper and we will get you started." He picked up the phone and spoke briefly to someone as Afiya's shaking hand scrawled her name.

At the sight of the contract with words she couldn't possibly comprehend, Afiya tasted terror in her throat. The room grew hazy, the air thick, everything spinning. She jumped to her feet, ready to bolt, when the man's voice caught her like a lash and hurled her back to earth.

"Sit down! We are giving you a job," the man ordered. "That is what you want, right? Walk out now, and you will never have a job with the government. Your family will starve! Is that what you want?"

Afiya sunk into the chair, defeated and confused. She started to cry.

The same haughty woman she met earlier now appeared, took Afiya by the arm, and ushered her to a waiting room. An older woman dressed in village garb was also there. Afiya wanted to ask what was going on, but she was too scared to utter a word. She clutched her paper bus ticket, the one that got her here, and wondered when this would all be over.

A man in a suit entered the room, ignored Afiya, and thrust a couple of bills at the older woman.

"This is what I can give you for the boy."

The woman stared at the money, lowered her head, took it from the man, and rushed from the room, her hands covering her face. Afiya thought she heard her crying.

A few minutes later, Afiya was led to another room where she sat for an hour. By now, she needed a bathroom, but who to ask? The haughty woman swept into the room, and before Afiya could speak, she was led outside to a windowless van. Afiya's heart pounded. In the grip of panic, she wet her underpants on the sidewalk, parting her legs to avoid her shoes. The woman made a sound of disgust, shoved her into the backseat, and slammed the door. Afiya huddled in the darkness, shaking in terror, recoiling at the smell of her own urine.

The ride finally stopped and the door opened. Blinded by sunlight, she smelled seawater, tar, and fish. She heard gulls calling and waves lapping against wood.

"Where are you taking me?" she begged the nameless stranger with rough hands and sour breath.

"You'll see," he said, laughing.

"Mom! I want my mom!" Afiya pleaded, but she was drowned out by more laughter.

Afiya, an innocent thirteen-year-old girl, was taken to a building on a pier and shoved into a small room where two hooded men waited. Over the next two days, she was beaten and raped dozens of times. The men screamed at her:

"Your parents don't love you."

"They sold you to us."

"This is your fault!"

"You should have been a better daughter!"

"This is all you're good for."

"You can never go home now."

"Who would want you after this?"

"You belong to us!"

She had never felt such pain. She couldn't move; when she tried to stand, her legs failed, every joint screamed, her skin was torn and bleeding, her muscles were in agony, deep bruises throbbed between blows. She was smeared with blood and sickening man-fluid; the stench of her violation revolted her twisted stomach. Shame and humiliation covered her like a shroud. There was nothing left of her will, of her identity. Her little-girl's heart was stripped naked and defenseless. Her mind broke. She became a shell, a useless body gutted for the lust of her voracious tormentors.

Deep down inside, she knew . . . this was all her fault; this was all she was good for; she could never return home now; she belonged to them.

She was in the world of sex trafficking.

Waking in her cage, Afiya continued crying. Eventually, a drunken deckhand appeared.

"Shu-up! Whatchu screaming about?"

Somewhere in Afiya's ravaged being, one last spark of hope appeared on the dark horizon.

"Please sir, a toilet. Please . . . help me. Kindness. Don't make me wet my blanket. I just need a toilet, and I will be quiet."

"Ah . . . a'right. . . . " slurred the deckhand. "C'mon. Jes' shu-up."

He thrust Afiya forward to the ship's head and stumbled, releasing his grip. Afiya darted past him, scaled a ladder to the upper deck, jumped onto the dock, and vanished into the night. The other caged children on the ship were not so lucky.

Afiya did not go to the police, nor did she return to her family. As fast as she fled, the shame and humiliation stayed with her. She spent several nights on the streets in blind panic, hiding from every stranger, snatching bits of discarded food scraps, coiled like a rat in a corner.

She eventually found her way to a church. It took all her strength to approach the door. The pastor and his wife took her to their home where she was fed, given new clothes, and counseled by mature women. She was safe . . . for now. The greater battle would come from within, and that would take years to overcome.

After several months, Afiya was enrolled in school and officially adopted by a family. Afiya's journey to healing would be a long one, but she is free and will find success.

Aftermath

Afiya narrowly escaped being shipped to Saudi Arabia where countless other children have disappeared. It is part of a thriving international trafficking ring. In fact, the last team that CRI sent to investigate sex trafficking in this nation reported that thousands of girls and boys have disappeared, and the state is either involved or is being paid to ignore it.

I have heard countless stories like Afiya's over my years of fighting this battle. International trafficking absolutely exists and is growing. Children are commodities, abused and transported around the globe. When I was working in Western Asia, we often intercepted girls being prepared to be shipped to the Middle East. In India, the traffickers go after Nepalese girls because their customers like the lighter-skinned girls. African girls are preferred by others. Of course, human trafficking is also on the rise in the US.

Human trafficking happens in many ways: clandestine border crossings, falsified shipping containers, private and commercial transportation such as boats, planes, trucks, and cars. As traffickers grow proficient at what they do, their profits soar. We need to get ahead of this vile, inhumane practice.

Human trafficking is a global contagion. Children like Afiya are in every country on the planet. Countless children and adults are waiting for the door of captivity to fly open and a champion to whisk them away to freedom. No child should suffer like the children who are trapped in darkness.

CRI is committed to fighting this evil, and by working with other organizations, law enforcement, governments, and key individuals, we will make a difference.

31

Survivor Care

The Heart of CRI

WHEN MOSES LED THE CHILDREN OF ISRAEL out of Egypt and through the Red Sea, he must have felt pretty good. Through obedience to God, he'd just prevailed over the most powerful despot on earth and watched as Egypt's army drowned in a miraculous feat of God's power. I imagine him thinking: "Rescue sorted. What's next?"

"What's next?" played out over the next forty years as the vestiges of slavery were expunged from the hearts and minds of the people. Recovery, it turned out, was not accomplished when Pharoah cried "Get your people out of here!" Nor was it realized on the dry bed of the Red Sea. The transformation from slaves to children of God was a miracle requiring time—and lots of it. It was in daily living that the true change occurred—something no miracle could accomplish.

When we rescue children from a brick kiln or brothel, our goal, from arrival to departure, is to complete the mission in eight minutes. Some rescues have taken longer, but fifteen minutes is about as long as we want to spend gathering victims, arguing with owners, and driving off with the precious lives.

The fact is, while our efforts have an immediate pay-off—the children are removed from the abusive environment—they still have a long way to go in their recovery.

Abused children like Afiya and Binsa have little chance of a normal life without the intervention of dedicated care-givers, carried out over several years. Yes, both children got out of slavery, but the damage done to them was deep-seated and pernicious.

At CRI, to rescue a child means more than extracting them from their abject circumstances. Generally, we will not free a child unless years of care can be provided. This is done in-country, through volunteers attending to their daily needs like food, shelter, clothing, school, medical care, and their emotional and spiritual needs as well. For the latter, trauma counselors are used where available.

Survivor Care is the strength of CRI's rescue efforts. Without it, our effectiveness as liberators would be nil, and it is quite likely that those we rescue would fall back into slavery. Reclaiming a destroyed life is not easy. The hard, cold facts are these: restoration of a child's innocence, their hope for a better life, and any dreams they may have had, takes years—even a lifetime. The need for healing is deep, even after physical deliverance from it. There are times when they are still caged in their minds and emotions, afraid to use the keys given to them for freedom. Physical removal from the trauma is the first step; emotional and mental deliverance can be ongoing. This is why CRI conducts follow-up health and wellness assessments of the children that they place in foster care.

Every culture is different in how they care for their children, so CRI's approach must vary. In Pakistan, the community that the child belongs to automatically cares for the recovering children. In other cultures, outside intervention is required such as building orphanages, children's homes, and boarding schools.

For example, through Emanuel's influence, we can send rescued children to volunteer homes through village and church networks. The people are glad to do it. However, in G-man's country, the sense of community support is not prevalent, so CRI approaches aftercare differently.

We also realize that putting a child in a foster home or orphanage is not the end of our responsibility. While many children thrive in most homes, some do not. Sometimes, the host families have the best intentions but their resources are stretched. Other times, the rescued child is too much to handle.

We are realists. "You get what you inspect." Our commitment to survivor care involves regular visits to monitor the children's conditions. Through our local networks or sending CRI people from the United States, we try to conduct a thorough audit of each child's home life every six months. This can vary with conditions and available resources. These visits consist of forensic interviews alone with the children and then alone with the host parents. From there, we write a detailed report (six to eight pages on each child) and keep it on file. During these interviews, we are looking at several things:

- condition of the child
- condition of the home

- neighborhood—is it safe?
- hygiene practices
- access to medical care
- recreational resources
- influence of other children or adults living in the home
- quality of the child's education

As we interview a child, we monitor their body language. Generally, we see lively children, bright and interested in life. We ask questions about their favorite food, their favorite color, how they like school. Their reactions to these questions are telling, and again, usually positive. However, if we ask about the past—their experiences in abusive environments—their body language tells a different story. The children grow quiet, draw in their arms and legs, and shutdown. It's horrifying to see, and we don't press it. It does, however, allow us to gauge the depth of their trauma and their need for specialized care.

The key to these interviews is trust, getting people to open up to us. We are there to help.

In one home, the children seemed happy and thriving, but they mentioned getting frequent headaches and dizziness. Further inquiry revealed that the host parents had a limited food budget due to school expenses. The children simply were not getting enough food. Working through our local resources, we arranged for additional financial help.

In another instance, G-man visited Binsa and some other girls to see how they were doing in their new home. As he sat and spoke with the girls, they told him of school, of playing with other children, and how they helped around the house. Binsa wore a purple shirt (her favorite color) and talked about how much she liked living there. She told G-man that she is getting good grades in school and she wants to be a teacher someday. She was also singing at her church—turns out she has a lovely voice. Binsa and the two other girls, also former slaves, were doing well and slowly becoming children again. Restoration of their innocence, their hope for a better life, and any dreams they had for themselves will take years to restore. With love and care, they will be able to slowly lose the grime and slime of evil.

Survivor Care makes this possible.

One of our most satisfying moments comes when a rescued child decides to become a liberator of children in their country. We realize that our efforts alone will not eradicate slavery, but if we can effect a culture shift, slavery will end. That is the greater goal. That shift begins with rescued children returning to the slave fields to fight injustice.

One such child is Mahima. In November 2017, Mahima was rescued from the atrocities of slavery in Southeast Asia. She was placed into a loving children's home where she lived with fifteen other girls who were also rescued from slavery. Soon after, Mahima expressed a desire to become a lawyer and fight trafficking in her country. At seventeen years old, she was in her second year of college. (In her culture, college begins in eleventh grade.) She is currently twenty-two. Her dream is to bring justice and to help other children who have gone through the same things she endured in slavery. It will take her two more years to complete her degree.

Mahima has an extraordinarily beautiful heart and wants to be an advocate for others who have no voice—those who have escaped the darkest of places.

This is what we call success.

Team member Ginsu, Professor, and a local woman wash off a newly rescued boy.

32

CRI Teams Training

Why are you here?

IT'S 7 A.M. ON A COOL JULY MORNING in upstate Pennsylvania. Two dozen men and women in athletic garb, knee braces, and headbands line up at the edge of a twenty-acre mowed field. Their shoes glisten with morning dew, grass clippings cling to their ankles, their limbs are shivering—ready to start. They are in their twenties and thirties, a few relics in their forties; they are bankers, real estate developers, missionaries, business people, retired military, a couple of ripped bodybuilders, a few slender computer geeks, one or two smokers, and a health food nut.

The burning sun that cleared the horizon two hours ago now glares at these students with unflinching objectivity. Who will make it? Who will give up first? Who will cough and puke? Who will cry?

"Why are you here?" screams an instructor, a barrel-chested former Marine. "You think this is gym class? Well, you're wrong. We are here to save children. What are you here for?"

The students respond to the orders of the cadre of instructors arrayed before them, but their attention is down range, some hundred yards away.

"Who will make it across?" roars an instructor, pacing back and forth like a hungry lion. "And who will fail their teammates? Okay, buddy up!"

Teams of two are quickly formed. Men with men, women with women, size for size. They stand together, shuffling their feet like thoroughbreds resisting the stalls, eager to run but nervous to start.

They are candidates to join Children's Rescue Initiative. For a week, they will be trained and tested, both in the field and in classrooms, by a cadre of instructors who are former military and active liberators combatting modern slavery. Classes include first-aid, land navigation, surveillance, S.E.R.E., self-defense, personality profiles, team dynamics, and rescue operations. Students are taught how to pick locks, escape hand restraints, detect a lie, navigate terrain, and recognize and rescue trafficked children.

At this moment, however, midweek into their training, the students are not thinking about tumblers or compasses. They don't care about breakfast in a few hours. They are focused on getting their partners to the other end of the grassy field.

"Fireman's carry. Now!" barks an instructor.

Twelve grunting students hoist their partners over their backs and shoulders, staggering to maintain balance in the slippery turf.

"You're in a burning building. Your partner's injured. It's up to you to save him. Run!"

And they're off. Stumbling, tumbling, fighting to stay upright. A line of separation quickly forms. A few sweaty, heaving bodies reach the finish in prime form. Several others struggle and receive kind words of encouragement from the sympathetic instructors.

"Get up!"

"You gonna drop me too?"

"What are you going to do when this is real?"

"You gonna quit in the field? Just quit now!"

Anyone who thought this training was conditioning quickly realizes their mistake. This is an evaluation, and not everyone is going to make it.

A line of stragglers slowly forms at the other end of the field, wet and grass-covered, hunched over, fighting for breath, cheering on the slower among them, awaiting their next task. Some venture back into the field, surround those still grinding it out, and shout encouragement.

When all teams reach the end, the roles are reversed. The carried are now the carriers and are ordered to hustle back to the starting line. Again, the stalwart few accomplish it with grace and determination. Those who struggled are now near collapse. Remarkably, the teams of women excel.

At the end of the week, instructors will meet to determine who is selected for what roles and who is rejected. Students are evaluated for overseas rescue missions and stateside support. Factors include a battery of tests on the final day of training. What have you learned? What can you do? What are you willing to do?

Just as the race is not always to the swiftest, the instructors are not looking for the strongest. They are looking for dedication, drive, instinct, acumen; they are looking for heart.

The teams continue up and down the field for hours, being made to crawl and drag their partners in different scenarios. They are soaked, dirty, and rebellious toward their own inadequacies. Fear and pain give way to purpose-driven action. A few quit, some puke, but most press on, smelling of green grass and sweat, muscles jellied and no longer viable, sinews pulling, bone against bone, clenched throats uttering guttural cries. A few flashback to their bootcamp days. "Sir, yes sir!" cries a Marine veteran.

The instructors bark orders and stare into blank eyes. They know the students are far away by now. They have been pushed beyond their limits, to the exact place intended. They are no longer excelling for themselves or the harpies demanding performance. They are excelling for each other.

"I love you, man," cries a team member, hugging the guy who just dragged him through a football field of grime and torment. This bond will last beyond the embrace. It will carry forth into fields of torture where humans are sacrificed for pleasure, where children's lives are commodities, where the nefarious reign, where the dregs of humanity rise unchecked to rule the dung heap, where challengers are few, where Satan revels, and evil rewards its minions. It will carry these liberators through the toughest times: the burning buildings, the jungle trails, the brickfields soaked in blood, the brothels pedaling innocent lives. It will carry them for a lifetime.

Evaluations come and go. The instructors know this. What they don't know is how each woman, each man, will perform under stress. Who will approach their weakness as an opportunity? Who will face their humanity and risk all on the journey of a lifetime? Who will join body and soul to the allegiance of dedicated liberators freeing the weakest among us?

Why are you here?

It is a question for all of us.

Why . . . ?

For we are all that stands between the monsters and the weak.

Boys are made to run back and forth all day hauling string to be braided into ropes. They are beaten daily and have little food.

33

A Clarion Call

The mandate for all free people is to become liberators of those enslaved. Our modern society has grown comfortable to the point of apathy while slavery has become the very fabric of many economies. This is no time for complacency, but for action by the free world to destroy this evil structure. Men and women like Frederick Douglass, William Lloyd Garrison, Sojourner Truth, Harriet Beecher Stowe, John Brown, Harriet Tubman, and William Wilberforce are just a few of the brave abolitionists who fought against slavery in our country and others, often at great peril, and often alone. Yet they freed their nation. Now other nations await more abolitionists.

Moses was a simple man, by all accounts an average man, but he had a call that was far greater than himself and his natural abilities—the call to free a nation.

Like many people of the western world, Moses lived a life of luxury separated from those suffering in slavery. Even though he was a Hebrew, he was raised in Pharaoh's palace—the seat of opulence and power. No doubt, he had heard of his people's suffering. At some point in his young life, he ventured beyond the palace walls to see it firsthand. It was this choice that led him to witness an

Egyptian beating a Hebrew slave. At that moment, something changed in him. Moses made a decision to help his people, risking everything: his wealth, status, health, and his very life to become a freedom fighter.

Moses's journey to set a nation free was not easy. Freedom fighters today face similar obstacles and persecution. Like Moses, danger lurks around every corner. Indeed, the mission of liberation is for the stubborn, the rebellious, the outcast—anyone willing to lay down their comforts to invade the horrific world of slave labor.

Moses did not liberate a nation overnight. Pharaohs do not go down easily nor give up their kingdoms without a fight. There is a Moses mindset that must be established in those called to be liberators. It is a mindset to be resilient, steadfast, stubborn, tenacious, and relentless for the mission. The thought of children in slave fields, men and women used like cattle, girls robbed of hope and life—must stay fresh in the mind lest one sinks back into the callous mindset of Pharoah and his rich nation.

Because of the radical change in Moses's life, he was willing to give up everything and accept hardship. In return, he was able to confront the most powerful ruler in the known world, face an economic system dependent on slavery, and put his life on the line for the Hebrew nation desperate for a leader. In the battle of strength against the evil leader, Moses saw the gradual breaking of Pharaoh's will until he practically begged Moses to take his people away. Through this struggle, Moses stood strong in his mission. In the end, millions of newly freed slaves plundered Egypt's treasures and walked away from their lives of bondage.

There is a movement today of ordinary people who are willing to step into the arena of danger and liberate those who have no rights, no voice, no hope, and most likely. . .no future.

So, the question remains. Will you take up the cause of justice and make a difference in this world? You don't need to be ex-military or some extraordinarily trained or gifted human. All you need is a passion and desire to do something. God can take an ordinary human and equip them to do extraordinary things. You don't need to be the smartest or fastest, just obedient to a higher call—one much bigger than yourself.

You can spend your life in a safe zone, or you can live your life having a lasting impact. And then there is the comfort zone. The comfort zone is really a killing zone. When we settle for comfort, many times our dreams and goals are killed. Many people have been lulled to sleep in the pursuit of comfort only to find sorrow at the end of their lives, realizing that their life has meant nothing. Embrace the discomfort zone and make a difference!

You can be a champion. The children of the world need an army of warriors that refuse to give up until children are liberated.

The call to action is to stand strong against evil. We live in a day and age where we need champions committed, compelled, and courageous, finding their cause in bringing justice where darkness is invading.

My hope is that when people arise to this mission of modern-day abolition, we will not only free slaves but will finally break the back of slavery and the systems that view humans as soulless commodities.

Are you ready to change someone's world?

. . . Assuredly, I say to you, inasmuch as you did it to one of the least of these My brethren, you did it to Me.

Matthew 25:40

About the Author

BRUCE LADEBU spent twenty years as a professional adventurer, explorer, and guide traveling to some of the wildest places on Earth, including first ascents in the Arctic and an expedition on the polar ice cap. He also spent time over three winters in the Canadian Rockies following and photographing wolves and other wildlife. He has guided hundreds of clients in climbing, survival, wilderness expeditions, and other adventure sports.

Since then, Bruce has started a number of organizations and has spoken in and advised leaders in many nations. He has extensive training in tactical skills and has trained in multiple combative arts, including Krav Maga, Silat, and Systema. He has completed two multi-week courses in executive protection.

He has also spoken in thirty-five nations, sharing powerful gospel truth as a Christian.

In the early nineties, Bruce traveled through the former Soviet Union countries and saw the terrible conditions children were forced to live in, including the marketing of young girls and boys forced into sex trafficking. Then in 2009, after witnessing labor slavery firsthand, Bruce worked to develop a strategy to rescue these individuals, and Children's Rescue Initiative was formed. As of April 2022, Bruce and his teams have rescued thousands of children and adults from labor slavery/sex trafficking and given them a start at a new life.

He's working on a second book about his life story.
To learn more or find out how you can help, contact Bruce through Facebook Messenger, or at:

Bruce@thechildrensrescue.org

CALL TO ACTION
Donate on the website
www.thechildrensrescue.org

Text "give" to 814-545-2360

Mail a check to
Children's Rescue Initiative
10670 PA-18
Conneaut Lake, PA 16316

rebel
queen

We hope you loved Bruce's book as much as
we have loved partnering with him in preparing it
for you! He is an inspiration and we hope you
have answered his call to action.

With a combined 20+ years in publishing,
we know how to help *anyone* write, launch,
and market a book. So if a book is on
your bucket list, we're the team to take it
from brain dump to bestseller.

RebelQueen.co
marti@rebelqueen.co
Facebook and Instagram @rebelqueenbooks